# PRINCIPLES OF SOCIAL STUDIES

## The Why, What, and How of Social Studies Instruction, Second Edition

James L. Barth
Kenneth Craycraft
Perry Marker
Jacquelin Stitt
Larry D. Wills
Sheila Wineman

UNIVERSITY
PRESS OF
AMERICA

LANHAM • NEW YORK • LONDON

All University Press of America books are produced on acid-free
paper which exceeds the minimum standards set by the National
Historical Publications and Records Commission.

# FOREWARD

The field of social studies did not exist even eighty years ago. Believe it or not a few of the early founders and leaders in the field are still productive social studies educators. Perhaps knowing that the field is newly defined and organized will help you to understand why there still remains so many unanswered questions about the very nature of the social studies.

In many ways, a social studies methods book reflects the turmoil, the arguments, the lack of unity that the field is just beginning to overcome. This methods book not unlike others in the field reflects a particular set of biases. The authors have definite priorities which have shaped this book into their image. There are ideas, skills, practices, activities that you should know before teaching the social studies. We the authors believe that knowing and practicing the social studies as offered in the following chapters will help you and ultimately your students to reach the social studies goal of citizenship education.

We have organized the book into three major parts. Part I, "Why Social Studies Education?" leads you to examine the field with special emphasis on identifying the meaning of social studies. "Now that I Know Why, What Do I Do?" Part II, emphasizes definitions, methods, skills and specific techniques of instruction. The final Part III, "Putting It All Together or How Do I Do It?" introduces planning of units and daily lesson plans with special emphasis on how to evaluate curriculum materials followed by units on giftedness, mainstreaming, and multi-cultural education.

No book such as this text is ever the exclusive work of the authors for they have drawn from the scholarship and inspiration of past social studies educators. We owe a debt to colleagues who have encouraged the authors to write a text that reflects their priorities. In particular we wish to recognize the contribution of the College of Education at Bowling Green State University and the Department of Education at Purdue University.

West Lafayette, Indiana
Fall, 1983

James L. Barth

This book is dedicated to three Ohio
social studies educators who through
their teaching and scholarship have
significantly contributed to the
field.
  Edgar B. Wesley
  Alan Griffin
  Robert E. Jewett

# CONTENT

Foreward

## PART I:  WHY SOCIAL STUDIES EDUCATION?

## INTRODUCTION

Did you ever ask yourself, "Why did I have to take social studies"?  As students, most of us have.  This is especially true as we sit through many boring lessons on the discoverers, establishment of Jamestown, or major battles of the Civil War.  We memorized the names of the Great Lakes, the three principal products of Brazil, and filled in the names of the fifty states on a map.

But, did you ever ask your teacher why you had to do all this?  If so, what do you think would have been the answer?  Some typical responses:  "You have to know this to be passed on to the next grade."  "It makes you think."  "You will be able to use this information when you are an adult."  "It is in the book, and it is important."  "It will be on the test."  Some may have said, "Any informed citizen should know these things if you are going to be an intelligent citizen."  What other answers have you heard?  List below:

1.

2.

3.

The problem is few teachers or students have really sat down to determine the goal of social studies in any systematic fashion.  Typically, the textbook determines what is to be taught.  At the secondary school level, the teacher is given a text at the beginning of the year, and that determines the curri-culum.  Chapter two follows Chapter one, and so on.  At the elementary level, social studies is taught when other "basics" have been covered.  If social studies is included, it is as a frill or side activity to that which is "really" important.

Traditionally, social studies has been justified as that part of the curriculum which directly contributes to the goal of citizenship education. Citizenship is perceived as that time of life when school is over and the students are out in the "real" world making a living and raising their families. It is a time when they are doing those things expected in a democratic society.

If such is the goal of social studies, do our practices in the classroom actually develop those skills necessary to function in our society? Are we developing those attitudes and values supposedly important in a democratic society? What about the content of our social studies classes? Should such questions be asked if one thinks of citizenship education in terms of some future happening?

However, are these the only kinds of questions we should ask? As long as we continue to couch social studies as something which contributes to adulthood, we are overlooking the fact that our students are citizens at present, and what are we doing to develop their effectiveness as present-day citizens? Such questions as "What requirements are presently imposed on my students as citizens?" or, "What is effective citizenship for a third grader or twelfth grader?" These questions might add an extra and more meaningful dimension to our conception of social studies education.

Another consideration we might make is in the area of values and attitudes. If we believe social studies is citizenship education, what kinds of belief structures should be included in our curriculum? What is right and what is wrong? Is it left to the teacher to determine the values their students should hold? What is the role of the student in this process?

Have you ever thought about teaching students to participate in decision-making? Do you have a responsibility to help your student apply knowledge, skills and values through active participation in society? Even if you thought you had such a responsibility have you ever questioned the meaning of the words "active participation in society?" Does participation mean talking about issues in class, does it mean bringing the real world of social decision-making into the class? Does it perhaps mean leaving the classroom to participate in the real political world outside the school? Knowledge, skills, values and participation, all of these may be the basic ingredients of proper citizenship education.

PART I.:  UNIT 1

## SOCIAL STUDIES AS CITIZENSHIP EDUCATION
Larry D. Wills

What we might do now is to ask ourselves, "What is my definition of citizenship"?  Hopefully, such considerations should be made in light of what we mean by "good" citizenship.  In order for us to come to terms with various concepts of citizenship education, perhaps we can begin by asking such questions as (1) What should my students know in order to become "good" citizens? (2) What skills are necessary in order to function in our society? and (3) What attitudes  and values may be needed to function in present-day society?

When asking such questions, we are beginning to form our curriculum objectives with reference to citizenship education.  The important element is that we have coupled our goals with the "why" of social studies education.  Until we have answered the "why" of social studies, we may become embroiled in a seeming mindlessness of curriculum development that leads us in all directions with no clear focus.

First, let us consider knowledge or content.  In your undergraduate teacher education program, you have been taking courses in the various social sciences plus coursework in such areas of math, science, humanities, and the fine arts.  Did you ever ask why you were asked to take such courses?  These courses do represent the scholarly endeavors of social scientists, mathematicians, etc.  They represent the "structure of knowledge" peculiar to particular disciplines of thought.  In the social studies, we are primarily concerned with the knowledge accumulated by the social scientists, but we do not ignore the findings in other disciplines.  For the moment, however, let us focus on knowledge typically found in the social sciences, such as history, sociology, political science, etc.  In sociology, for example, much attention is placed on the way people act in groups.  We know that we behave in various group settings which include primary and secondary groups.  We also know that people tend to exhibit certain ethnocentric behavior.  What one person accepts as natural, another would accept as strange.

Space does not allow us to deal with any depth in any one of the social sciences, but keep in mind we will utimately have to deal with the selection of content. We will have to consider those facts, concepts, and generalizations deemed worthwhile in citizenship education.

Secondly, what skills are we going to identify as crucial in citizenship education? For example, is it necessary for our students to be able to determine what is fact and what is opinion? Are there any particular reading skills necessary for our students to function in a democratic society? The list might also include such skills as map reading or reasoning skills.

Third, what kinds of attitudes and values are worthwhile? Should we focus on developing a respect for the law or the right of privacy? Should we encourage our students to respect differing viewpoints or differing life styles?

To start your thinking identify for me in the space provided below the type of content, the specific skills and the proper attitudes/values which should be part of a citizenship education program.

Content:

Skills:

Attitudes/Values:

Knowledge, skills, and attitudes/values should not be developed in isolation to reality. Too frequently our students do not see the relevancy of their classroom activities to the world in which they live. In order to encourage students to use what they learn in the classroom, they should be involved in various forms of social participation. In a democracy, we should be committed to the worth of the individual, and actions of citizens in our society should be directed to the resolution of social conflicts with the maintenance of human dignity for all.

As noted in the Introduction to this Chapter, students are citizens now. With this perspective, how can we actively involve them in some form of social participation? In the space provided below, suggest possible ways in which students can be involved in social action projects:

1. Interviewing public officials.

2.

3.

In Unit I, objectives in social studies have focused on knowledge, skills, attitudes/values and social participation. At this time, write your own definition of social studies education. In Unit II, one can compare his/her defintion with others in the field.

Student's definition of social studies is:
(Write your definition in the space provided below)

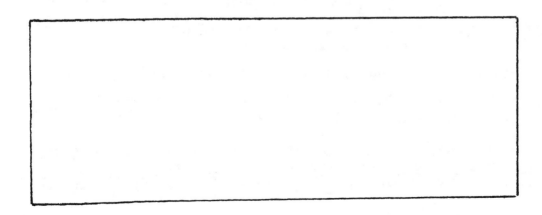

PART I: UNIT 2

## DEFINITION, GOAL, PURPOSES, AND TRADITIONS OF THE SOCIAL STUDIES*

James L. Barth

The field of social studies was, until recent years, unique to the United States. Only within the last decade have other nations begun to adopt social studies as a description of their programs for citizenship education. Social studies began to evolve in American schools early in the 20th Century and in many ways reflects the changing values, attitudes, and beliefs of Americans.

A review of the history of the social studies movement suggests that there have been historical trends toward certain points of view about how social studies ought to be taught. One the one hand scholars, boards and commissions have pronounced their visions of what social studies ought to be, and on the other hand classroom teachers have had their visions of what they ought to be teaching. In other words, the field of social studies exists but there continues to be within the field significant disagreement as to definition and meaning.

Historically the American educational system had always offered history, some form of social sciences, and the humanities such as philosophy as separate subjects, but it was not until social studies that substantial attempts were made to integrate the social sciences, history and the other humanities for the purpose of instruction in citizenship education. So in brief, some of the key ideas about the field have to do with citizenship and the integration of knowledge.

### A Definition of What Social Studies Is

Social studies is the integration of
experience and knowledge concerning
human relations for the purpose of
citizenship education.

"Integration" is emphasized for social studies is the only field which deliberately attempts to draw upon, in an integrated fashion, the data of the social sciences and the insights of the humanities. "Citizenship" is

*This chapter was originally published in Methods of Instruction in Social Studies Education, by James L. Barth (Washington, D.C.: University Press of America, 1979). It has been revised for purposes of this text.

emphasized for social studies, despite the difference in orientation, outlook, purpose and method of teachers, is almost universally perceived as preparation for citizenship in democracy.

This definition takes into consideration the competing notions of the goal of social studies. The definition is not to be conceived as the final definition for social studies is a movement. A definition merely reflects the accumulation of ideas about the field at this moment in time. Ideas about the meaning of social studies have evolved from a definition that claimed it was to be only a collection of separate but related subjects to a claim that it was merely the social sciences simplified for pedagogical purposes to the present statement that "social studies is the integration of experience and knowledge concerning human relations for the purposes of citizenship education."

## Social Studies Curriculum Based Upon Goals and Purposes

Schools do have a social studies curriculum K-12 and as part of the curriculum the school offers history, sociology, economics, civics, problems of democracy, senior problems, government, values and issues, global international studies, etc. Social studies implies that there are common general purposes that link the separate social sciences and humanities to a concept of citizenship. Schools are now attempting to coordinate their K-12 social studies curriculum toward commonly agreed upon goals and purposes with the hope of developing a consistent citizenship education program.

## Social Studies Educators Agree on a Goal and Objectives

Most social studies educators and classroom teachers seem to agree that social studies ought to be integration and further that the purpose has something to do with citizenship. What teachers have is a variety of different interpretations of how the school should promote good citizenship.

So, what do social studies educators believe? They believe that citizenship education is the goal of social studies. Further than that they may also have general common agreement, evolved through practice and usage, on some of the objectives by which the goal of citizenship education is to be accomplished. For example, there is considerable agreement about the following four objectives; that is, if teachers were to reach these objectives, they would have reached the goal of citizenship. These four objectives (<u>Social</u> <u>Studies</u> <u>Guidelines</u> Washington, D.C.: National Council for the Social Studies, 1971) are in terms of what students should be taught.

1. Knowledge about the human condition which includes past, present, and future.

2. Skills necessary to process information.

3. Skills to examine values and beliefs.

4. The application of knowledge through active participation in society.

## <u>Disagreement</u> <u>on</u> <u>the</u> <u>Meaning</u> <u>and</u> <u>Application</u> <u>of</u> <u>Goal</u> <u>and</u> <u>Objectives</u>

In other words, educators believe that social studies teachers, if asked, would agree that the <u>four</u> <u>objectives</u> above are significant means of achieving the goal of citizenship, that these are objectives that they would attempt to teach. If, as suggested, teachers agree to the goal and to at least four objectives by which to accomplish the goal of social studies, then what specifically is it that they disagree about? It is believed that their disagreement is on the meaning of citizenship and on the application of the four objectives.

It is agreed that students ought to <u>gain</u> <u>knowledge</u>, a means of <u>pro-</u> <u>cessing</u> <u>information</u>, skills to analyze values, and to practice <u>participation</u>. The disagreement is on what knowledge should be learned, what is the best way to process information, how best to examine values, and what is meant by participation. So, to summarize, there is agreement on the words citizen- ship, processing, valuing, and participation; there is disagreement on mean- ing and application.

## <u>Three</u> <u>Traditions</u> <u>Approach</u> <u>to</u> <u>Clarifying</u> <u>Meaning</u>

So, as has been said, there are points of agreement and disagreement. To think clearly about where the movement has been, where it is now, and where it is going, some set of organizing ideas is needed to help clarify the agreements and disagreements. The <u>Three</u> <u>Traditions</u> approach to organi- zing ideas is one of the more promising ways to clarify and summarize the meaning of citizenship and the four objectives. For a clear and concise development of the Three Traditions approach see: Barr, Barth, and Shermis, <u>The</u> <u>Nature</u> <u>of</u> <u>the</u> <u>Social</u> <u>Studies</u> (Palm Springs, CA: ETC Publications, 1978); also Barr, Barth and Shermis, <u>Defining</u> <u>the</u> <u>Social</u> <u>Studies</u> (Washington, D.C.:

National Council for the Social Studies, 1977); and Barth, Elementary and Middle School Social Studies Curriculum Program, Activities, and Materials (Washington, D.C.: University Press of America, 1979).

## Purpose, Method and Content

Identifying the three different traditional ways that social studies has been taught resulted from considering certain basic questions about events that makeup the social studies movement. These basic questions are those which teachers ask themselves before they teach: (1) What is my purpose? (2) How will I teach (method)? (3) What content should I teach? As these three basic teaching questions were applied to the field, it was found that essentially there were three traditional ways that teachers had taught social studies and that these traditions could be rather clearly identified: Social Studies taught as Citizenship Transmission, Social Studies taught as Social Science and History, and Social Studies taught as Reflective Inquiry. The reason they have been called traditions is that they have been part of the social studies movement for the past seventy years. It has never been said that the three traditions were the only possible ones to emerge for there are undoubtedly others. What is believed is that the three traditions are the major ones, that is, most social studies classroom teachers and social studies educators could find themselves supporting one of these three traditions. The differences between the traditions on purpose, method and content are identified in this chart. Originally published in Defining the Social Studies by Barr, Barth, and Shermis, the chart has been modified for publication in this book.

## Reading the Chart

When reading the chart ask yourself with which statement do I agree? Do I agree with the first, the second or the third. The chart offers three choices (three different ways of teaching social studies). Which one of the three would I (the reader) choose as the tradition most agreeable to my way of thinking.

The Three Social Studies Traditions

|  | 1<br>Social Studies<br>Taught as Citizen-<br>ship Transmission | 2<br>Social Studies<br>Taught as Social<br>Science | 3<br>Social Studies<br>Taught as Reflective<br>Inquiry |
|---|---|---|---|
| Purpose | Citizenship is best promoted by <u>incul-cating "right"</u> values as a frame-work for making decisions. | Citizenship is best promoted by decision-making based on mas-tery of social science concepts, processes and problems. | Citizenship is best promoted through a process of inquiry in which knowledge de-rives from what citi-zens need to know to make decisions and solve problems. |
| Method | <u>Transmit</u><br>Transmission of concepts and val-ues by such tech-niques as text-book, recitation, lecture, question-answer and problem exercise. | <u>Discovery</u><br>Each social sci-ence has its own method of gather-ing and verifying knowledge. Stu-dents should dis-cover the disci-pline's problems through a struc-ture that is ap-propriate to each social science. | <u>Reflective Inquiry</u><br>Decision-making is structured and disci-plined through re-flective inquiry pro-cess which aims at responding to con-flicts by means of testing insights. |
| Content | Content is selec-ted by an author-ity interpreted by the teacher and has the function of illustrating values, attitudes and beliefs. | Proper content is the structure, concepts, pro-blems and pro-cesses of both the separate and the integrated social science disciplines | Analysis of indivi-dual citizen's values yields need and inter-ests, which in turn, form the basis for student self-selection of problems. Problems therefore, constitute the content for re-flection. |

<u>Interpretation of the Chart</u>

Purpose

All three traditions accept citizenship as the purpose but they signi-ficantly disagree as to how best to achieve the purpose. Citizenship Trans-mission (CT), the oldest and most practiced tradition, would have the teacher indoctrinate certain right behavior, whereas Social Science (SS) tradition would have students concentrate on mastery of social science and history content, and Reflective Inquiry (RI) focuses on a process of inquiring about personal social problems. The point is that each of the three traditions approaches the act of teaching in a different way. One says, "I'll tell you what's right." Another says, "Here are 'good' social science concepts and problems." And a third says, "The process of identifying and verifying knowledge based upon the citizen's values, needs, and interests is really most important."

## Method

Some teachers looking at these three traditions will say, "Let's be eclectic. Take what you like from each of the three and that is the way we ought to teach social studies to achieve citizenship." An interesting thought, but at the present it just should not be done for the simple reason that the beliefs in one position are diametrically opposed to those of another. Take the category method--the CT emphasizes the uncritical transmission of concepts and values that are couched as simple problem-solving exercises such as are found at the end of text chapters, i.e., What important advice did Washington give the nation in his Second Inaugrual Address? What were the three main reasons for entering World War I?

Method for SS is called discovery. Understand that the social scientists have a structure of knowledge and that structure is knowable. The student is expected to use that structure to discover relationships between events. The student is to discover what the teacher or text already knows. It's very simple--the teacher has the answer behind his/her back. When students discover (through a discovery process, scientific method), the teacher reveals the hidden answer and says, "Yes, you've discovered the right relationship." The learning theory supporting this method assumes students are thrilled at having found the right relationships. One final important point, SS identifies the problems, that is, the problem the student will study is identified and approved by the discipline, i.e., Should civil disobedience be tolerated in a democratic society? What is the social stratification in Nigeria? What impelled William the Conqueror to invade England? How does scarcity theory help explain the problem of inflation?

RI teachers look upon transmission and discovery methods with disdain because they believe that the best method is that of an inquiry process through which students identify and study significant social, personal problems. In other words, the best way of solving life's problems is through disciplining one's thinking through reflective inquiry. Reflective Inquiry is a process that requires students to identify their values, needs, and problems for the purpose of making decisions on significant social, personal issues. Can you identify how RI and SS differ on "What is a problem?" It is not just a small difference, it is a big one. SS would have one study problems identified by the discipline, in other words, the discipline owns the problem. Who owns the problem under the RI tradition, that is, who identifies and clarifies it? RI says the student must own the problem, for it is the student who is required to identify his/her own values and needs because felt social, personal problems arise from those needs and values. The most significant social studies, the RI would continue, is that which is based on those problems, needs and values of the student. It sounds like a little thing to say "Who owns the problem?" It's not. CT says the teacher should, SS says the discipline does, RI says the student must otherwise the problem is not relevant. Can you see why social studies teachers have difficulty communicating with each other? Most all social studies teachers believe in discussing social problems. The question is whose problem, the teacher's, the discipline's, or yours? This is one of the places where educators have not been able to reconcile their differences.

## Content

What about content? Do teachers agree on what content to teach? Not likely. If they cannot agree on purpose and method, they are not going to agree on content. The CT select those materials which illustrate the values, attitudes and beliefs they want their students to emulate. In practice this means selecting stories that illustrate the virtues of sharing, being kind to dogs, and the tragedy of war and automobile accidents. Proper content for the SS is the known concepts, generalizations, theories, processes, and problems of the separate social science disciplines (political science, geography, sociology, anthropology, economics, psychology, and history). Note how this differs from the CT content. The SS is not trying to find materials that will indoctrinate certain points of view, but to teach the essential structure of the social science discipline. Obviously the RI would seriously question the content of either CT or SS. Content should properly arise from values, needs, interests, and problems of students according to RI. How do the RIs see the world? They see people behaving in a particular way. The way one behaves depends upon one's values. One's values yield needs and interests. The needs and interests of one person might well conflict with the needs and interests of others. After all, we all recognize that there is, in fact, value conflict, so also there is a conflict between people's needs and interests. Those conflicts are called <u>problems</u>. It is logical, the RI contends, to think that the best social studies curriculum by which to teach citizenship is that which focuses on problems identified by students.

Some teachers have looked at the three traditions and have concluded that each citizen goes through all three traditions but at different times of life. For example, some believe that elementary teachers tend to emphasize citizenship training through a CT approach. Whereas some junior high and high school teachers who have been trained in the social sciences and history emphasize a CT/SS approach. Higher education emphasized the SS approach but the individual faced with the real world after graduation will integrate knowledge and follow an RI approach. There is probably some truth in the observation that students pass through certain different traditions. But that these traditions easily break into elementary, secondary, higher education and life is not probably all that clear-cut. Assuming for the moment there might be something to the argument that life beyond the formal structures of education is really one of problem-solving and decision-making, then perhaps you can understand why the RI advocates believe that they, among the three, are the most relevant to what people really do, to the problems they really have. For the RI curriculum, methods and purpose are all aimed at decision-making based upon reflection--teach children from kindergarten right through graduate school to inquire, for that is the best way of meeting the challenge of a modern complex, industrialized, interdependent society.

## The Three Traditions in Conflict With Each Other

All three traditions agree that citizenship education aimed at developing decision-makers is the best way to view the purpose for teaching social studies. They disagree on how that decision-making should be taught. Some

would try to combine the three traditions into one, but this is difficult
for each tradition does reject the purpose, method, and content of the other.
All three traditions have their points of argument. Surely it is true that
CT dominates the teaching of social studies in elementary and CT/SS in
secondary. SS is essentially found in higher education. RI claims to be
the position of the future, for as the society becomes more heterogeneous,
that is, as it becomes more problem oriented, the demand for an inquiry
approach to decision-making will become irresistible. If social studies
educators were to have their way, then the inquiry method would become the
accepted approach, but it is not at all clear that this is what will happen.
Perhaps a safer prediction would be that the three traditions would continue
until the end of this century to conflict with each other in their attempts
to dominate. In fact, social studies teachers cannot escape this conflict.
If you teach social studies you are part of this conflict, for either con-
sciously or by default you undoubtedly fall into one of the three traditions,
and though you may not be completely consistent with one tradition, it is
probable that you will support one over the others. So the future of the
three traditions belongs to you. Your purposes for teaching, your method,
your content, they will determine the future meaning of social studies for
your students.

## Summary on the Meaning of Social Studies

Social studies as a field has been part of education for well over half
a century. The decade has been one of struggle for social studies--its
meaning has never been clear, neither to those in the field not to those outside. Out of these years of conflict a definition has emerged that is broad
enough to include most all other definitions of social studies but yet narrow enough to have meaning:

> Social studies is the integration of
> experience and knowledge concerning
> human relations for the purpose of
> citizenship education.

This definition suggests that citizenship is the goal of social studies
instruction. Upon this most social studies educators agree. Also agreement
has been achieved on four general purposes which, if followed, will lead to
the education of "good citizens" according to the professional organization,
National Council for the Social Studies. It is upon the application of the

four purposes that educators disagree. That disagreement tends to fall into three distinct traditions: (1) social studies taught as Citizenship Transmission, (2) social studies taught as Social Science and History, (3) social studies taught as Reflective Inquiry. These three traditions help to explain how teachers can agree upon words such as gaining knowledge, processing information and participation, and yet differ significantly on the meaning of these words when they are applied to the teaching of citizenship. The social studies movement continues to grow and develop for despite constant wrangling, there is substantial agreement on what social studies ought to be and what it ought to accomplish. What supports this notion is the belief that social studies exists to teach future citizens <u>how</u> <u>to</u> cope with the problems arising out of 20th Century complexity and <u>how</u> <u>to</u> make decisions in a pluralistic technologically advanced self-governing society. On to the 21st Century.

Circle your Preference

Instructions: Circle the word or words that most nearly represent your beliefs:

1.  Which of the traditions would <u>you</u> <u>like</u> to follow?

    1. Social studies taught as citizenship transmission
    2. Social studies taught as social science
    3. Social studies taught as reflictive inquiry

2.  Which of the traditions have your experienced as a student?

    1. Social studies taught as citizenship transmission
    2. Social studies taught as social science
    3. Social studies taught as reflective inquiry

3.  Which of the traditions have you observed during field experience in the public schools?

    1. Social studies taught as citizenship transmission
    2. Social studies taught as social science
    3. Social studies tuaght as reflective inquiry

4.  Which tradition are you most likely to follow when you teach social studies as a certified teacher?

    1. Social studies taught as citizenship transmission
    2. Social studies taught as social science
    3. Social studies taught as reflective inquiry.

PART II: NOW THAT I KNOW, WHAT DO I DO?
INTRODUCTION

Can you be trusted with a secret? If you promise not to tell, well, then maybe you can be told. The secret is that most public classroom social studies teachers do not seem to be much interested in the question, "Why social studies?" They reason that some authority decided social studies should be part of the school curriculum, so teach it, what is there to know about it? Many teachers feel that they do not need to define a position, define a field, or know the teaching traditions in the field. I think that attitude is understandable, though from my point of view a bit narrow. Leave the questions of philosophy and theory, some teachers seem to feel, to those so-called authorities who write texts and attend conventions, for, in fact, a classroom social studies teacher just is not held responsible for such questions as Why social studies. We, classroom teachers, are held responsible for the application of theory to practice. We, the teachers, are faced with the very practical question, "What do we do on Monday morning?"

Did I hear you ask, "Are there some practical basic things I ought to know before I teach social studies?" Yes, of course there are some basic ideas, skills, and methods that you should be expected to know. Do you know the difference between a fact and a generalization? Can you conduct a class discussion using the four different levels of questioning? What is the difference between methods, techniques and strategies. Occasionally teachers use all three as though they were one and same, are they?

Part II, Now That I Know Why, What Do I Do? is the practical information, methods and skills which teachers say they want to know. This part will help you with the question, "What do I do and how do I do it on Monday morning?" Do you want to know how to ask four levels of questions, prepare an inquiry lesson, define a concept, write an objective, individualize a lesson, identify a hundred teaching techniques, including five types of grouping, and develop attitudes and values in social studies? Then the eleven units in Part II will be important to you.

Can I still trust you to keep our secret? Perhaps you are right, maybe it never was a real secret that Why never was quite so appealing to the classroom teacher as the practical question, How do I do it? Surely your first obligation is to that for which you are held responsible. You will need to know the content of Part II if you are to be responsible.

PART II: UNIT 1

## DEFINITIONS AND EXAMPLES OF FACTS, CONCEPTS AND GENERALIZATIONS
Jacquelin Stitt and Perry Marker

The discipline of social studies encompasses a variety of content areas, all of which involve the study of man as a social being living in his environment. In the content areas of history, political science, economics, sociology, psychology, anthropology, and geography, one finds vast amounts of information. In addition to these content areas within the discipline of social studies, one also finds other areas that contribute to and enhance the social studies, e.g. music, art, literature, science, etc. Combined, this information forms the knowledge base from which the social studies teacher operates.

Because of the wide range and vast amount of information encompassed by the social studies, it would be difficult, if not impossible, to teach, or expect students to learn, everything. Therefore, the process of selecting and organizing the information becomes vital. This process is called a content analysis.

In the content analysis, the teacher examines the available information, identifying the facts, concepts, and generalizations toward which instructional activities will be directed.

### Facts

Facts are statements that can be empirically verified through the information (textbooks, films, library resources, newspapers, magazines, etc.) available to the students. That is, factual statements contain information that can be identified as being true or false. Each statement is unique in itself, representing something that happened at a given time or place. Facts are specific in nature. Facts are the basic information from which content grows. It would be very difficult to understand the world of social studies if facts were not available. The following are examples of facts:

On April 30, 1970, the U.S. invaded Cambodia.

Abraham Lincoln was the sixteenth President of the U.S.

The capital of Ohio is Columbus.

While facts are the basis for the social studies, it is not always enough for students to memorize them. Rather, it is essential for students to understand the relationships between and among facts. Recognizing the relationships allows the student to organize the many facts and create meaning. Thus, students can acquire an understanding of events, individuals, and incidents that relate to their own experiences in, as well as out, of the classroom.

## Concepts

A concept can best be described as a grouping of facts. It is an abstract idea or interpretation based upon specific instances. Concepts are invented by the student after he/she has observed similarities among the facts. An example is:

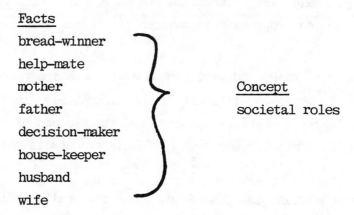

Facts
bread-winner
help-mate
mother
father
decision-maker
house-keeper
husband
wife

Concept
societal roles

In this example, the student reviews the list of facts and identifies each as a role an individual might fulfill in modern society. Bits and pieces of factual information are categorized to form concepts. The formation of concepts is necessary for learning to occur, but in order for a student to utilize the information in dealing with the world, he must form generalizations.

## Generalizations

Once concepts have been formed, relationships must be expressed to give them meaning. These relationships are referred to as generalizations. A generalization is a statement that can be applied to new situations. Generalizations provide insight into how society functions.

The facts and concept identified earlier related to roles. The generalization toward which these are directed might be: Every person is expected to play many roles in his/her lifetime. It is important, however, to note here that a single concept does not lead to a generalization. Additional concepts would be required in order to reach the generalization identified above. A fully developed content analysis for this generalization has been provided at the end of this chapter.

## Content Analysis

Content analysis is a technique that the teacher can use in preparing for instruction. The chart format used in the example at the end of this unit allows the teacher to identify the essential facts leading to the formation of each concept, as well as the concepts leading to the formation of the generalization. Unnecessary facts, which do not contribute to concept formation, can be eliminated. Facts not available to the students in a reading assignment can be provided through alternative strategies. Facts dispersed throughout a reading assignment can be collected so that instruction can be provided to assist the student in locating and organizing the related facts.

## Evaluation of Generalizations

Once a student arrives at a generalization, the quality of that generalization should be determined. The following criteria may be used in this evaluation:

1. Can the student apply this generalization to new situations?

2. Can the student use this generalization in evaluating new information?

3. Can the student use this generalization to synthesize concepts as they are formed in social studies and other disciplines?

4. Is the generalization biased?

5. Does the generalization change as it applies to different material?

20

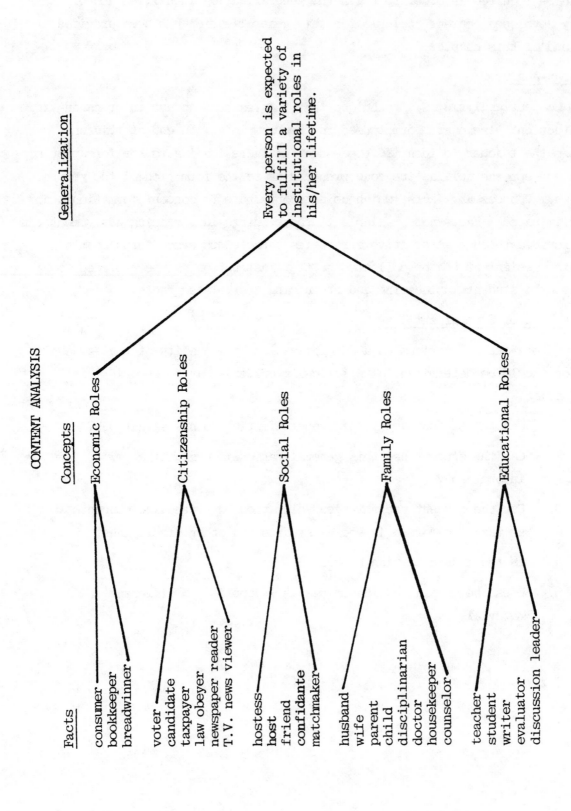

Generalization

Every person is expected to fulfill a variety of institutional roles in his/her lifetime.

CONTENT ANALYSIS

Concepts

Economic Roles

Citizenship Roles

Social Roles

Family Roles

Educational Roles

Facts

consumer
bookkeeper
breadwinner

voter
candidate
taxpayer
law obeyer
newspaper reader
T.V. news viewer

hostess
host
friend
confidante
matchmaker

husband
wife
parent
child
disciplinarian
doctor
housekeeper
counselor

teacher
student
writer
evaluator
discussion leader

ASSIGNMENT: Use this sample chart format to complete a content analysis for a unit. Evaluate the generalization you identify.

Generalizations

Concepts

Facts

PART II: UNIT 2

THE INTERDISCIPLINARY APPROACH

Jacquelin Stitt

The discipline of social studies seeks to develop concepts and generalizations which are related to, or shared by, other disciplines. The teaching of these concepts and generalizations often occurs at different times in the learning sequence of the various disciplines. (Examples of the disciplines are mathematics, science, language arts, etc.) The result is that students fail to see that one discipline is merely building upon or elaborating upon a concept or generalization already introduced in another discipline. Thus, students fail to see the relationship between their prior learning and the new learning which is occurring.

The interdisciplinary approach involves a conscious effort on the part of teachers* to assist students in recognizing the contributions of each discipline to the formation of a concept or generalization. This approach allows teachers to combine their resources in developing different aspects of the same concept or generalization. In an interdisciplinary approach, there is cooperative planning for instruction. The teachers representing each of the disciplines identify the concept or generalization to be developed jointly, the goal of instruction, the learning experiences that can be provided, and the different approaches that can be used. The interdisciplinary approach is the result of the combined contributions of the various disciplines: social studies, mathematics, language arts, science, fine arts, physical education and home economics.

## Webbing

A technique that is useful in planning for the interdisciplinary approach is WEBBING. The WEB can be likened to the outline, which is a linear presentation of ideas. This latter planning tool has often been used for instructional planning; each discipline is alternately listed, followed by the specific facts and learning activities related to the concepts and/or generalizations being developed. A simple format is followed:

I.   concept or generalization

    A.   fact from a discipline

        1.   learning activity

        2.   learning activity

   B.   fact from a second discipline
      1.   learning activity
      2.   learning activity

One problem, however, is associated with the outline format - it is difficult to
see how each piece fits into the total interdisciplinary framework.  The web, as
the name suggests, resembles a spider's web.  Like the spider's web, the interdisciplinary planning web is arranged around a single focal point - the concept
or generalization that will be developed during instruction.  The web is an
attempt to tie together all the pieces.

   The first step for teachers interested in the interdisciplinary approach
is to identify the common concept of generalization toward which instruction
will be directed.  This should be a concept or generalization that would normally be developed in each of the respective disciplines or one that could
logically be included.

   After the concept or generalization has been identified, a single large
sheet of paper is used to web all the parts.  In the center of the paper, the
concept of generalization is listed.  On the perimeter of the paper, each
discipline that is to be involved in the interdisciplinary approach is identified.  This provides the framework for the web.  (See figure 1 on the next
page)

   The third step requires that the representative of each discipline speci-
fies his/her contributions to the topic.  The social studies teacher needs to
begin by identifying each of the content areas - history, geography, sociology,
economics, psychology, and political science - and then, examining each to
determine the specific facts and concepts which can be contributed to the formation of the generalization.  Each of the teachers from the other disciplines
must also review the content areas encompassed by their disciplines to determine the facts and concepts which will contribute to the central generalization.
Through this process a complete web can be created.  It is quite possible that
the planning team will be able to make suggestions to one another; and it is
likely that other colleagues from the discipline will be able to make recom-
mendations.

24

(Figure 1)

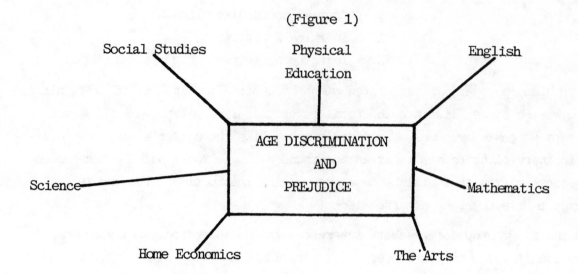

The social studies discipline has not made a contribution to the web in figure 2. Your assignment is to list the contributions (facts and concepts) that the social studies discipline can make to the generalization, "Age Discrimination and Prejudice." A web of the content areas in the social studies has been provided for this assignment (see figure 3).

After each discipline has identified the facts and concepts that relate to the generalization, the interdisciplinary team may wish to evaluate the total response. Facts and concepts which do not relate to the total understanding of the generalization can be eliminated; redundancy can be eliminated or reduced.

The fifth step is to identify activities that will enable students to learn. The teacher representing each discipline now reviews the facts and concepts listed on the web. He/she generates as many learning activities as possible that also will involve a variety of learning modalities. Once again colleagues, both in and out of the discipline, may be of assistance.

In figure 4, activities are listed for the discipline of language arts. Your assignment is to generate activities for social studies around the facts and concepts you identified in figure 3. Consult with another person in the class.

(Figure 2)

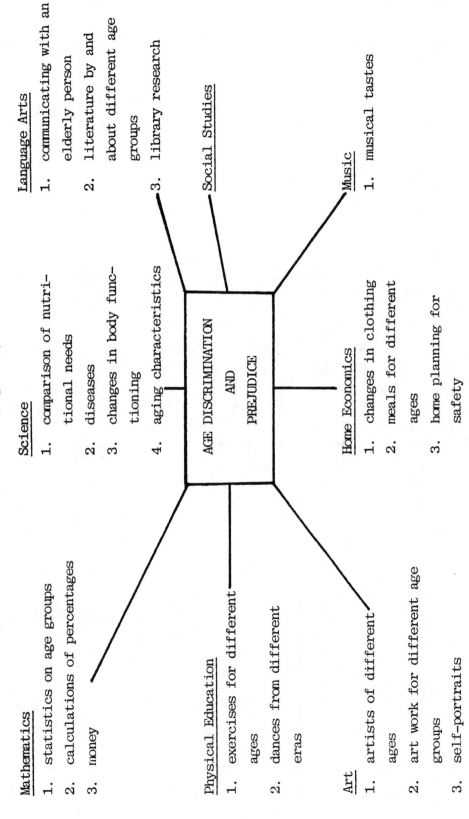

**Mathematics**
1. statistics on age groups
2. calculations of percentages
3. money

**Physical Education**
1. exercises for different ages
2. dances from different eras

**Art**
1. artists of different ages
2. art work for different age groups
3. self-portraits

**Science**
1. comparison of nutritional needs
2. diseases
3. changes in body functioning
4. aging characteristics

AGE DISCRIMINATION AND PREJUDICE

**Home Economics**
1. changes in clothing
2. meals for different ages
3. home planning for safety

**Language Arts**
1. communicating with an elderly person
2. literature by and about different age groups
3. library research

**Social Studies**

**Music**
1. musical tastes

26

(Figure 3)

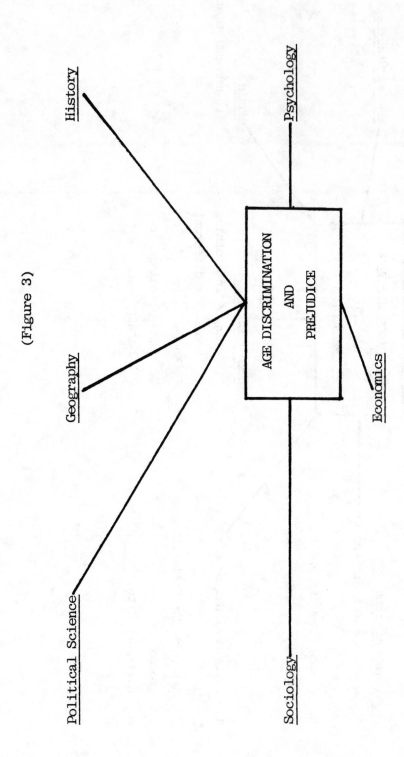

(Figure 4)

| Language Arts | Social Studies |
|---|---|

1.  communicating with an elderly
    person
    a.  talk with a grandparent
        about the things they
        did at your age
    b.  write a letter to someone
        in a nursing home, describing
        your activities
    c.  interview an elderly person
        to determine how they feel
        about the issues of the day

2.  literature by and about different
    age groups
    a.  read one of the books listed
        on the bibliography
    b.  share your favorite book with
        someone younger and someone
        older than you
    c.  identify the literary tech-
        niques used in books designed
        for different age groups
    d.  list stereotypes found in liter-
        ature of different age groups

3.  library research
    a.  locate population statistics
        for age groups
    b.  develop a bibliography of
        magazines intended for
        different age groups
    c.  present a panel discussion
        on the topic, "You Can't
        Trust Anyone Over Thirty"

After each discipline has listed the activities, the teachers again review - this time the activities. Additional suggestions may be made for any
discipline by the instructional team. They are also expected to ascertain
that a variety of activities have been listed, including both active and
passive involvement and a variety of learning modalities. In instances involving duplication of activities, a decision should be reached as to who
will use the activity. Activities can be identified for use by each discipline during the time of the interdisciplinary teaching/learning experience.
A schedule of learnings can be established so that each instructor will be
aware of what is happening in his/her colleagues' classes on a particular day.

The interdisciplinary approach requires planning time on the part of
the instructional team. It cannot be accomplished without preparation. It
also requires evaluation as a follow-up, in order to determine if it is an
effective way of teaching for the instructional team.

Another requirement of the interdisciplinary approach is a positive attitude on the part of the teachers involved. No teacher should enter into this
type of arrangement unwillingly. Additionally, each teacher must be willing
to share his/her ideas with colleagues and accept the opinions of other.

*A single teacher can plan for the interdisciplinary approach -
in the elementary schools, one teacher is responsible for all
disciplines; in the secondary schools, one teacher is responsible for all content areas.

PART II:  UNIT 3

METHODS, TECHNIQUES AND STRATEGIES*

James L. Barth

Purpose:  Having read this chapter, you should be able to compare and contrast active vs. passive teaching, identify the differences between method, strategies and techniques, and identify seven active learning techniques.

## Introduction

Some authorities believe that there are only two general methods of teaching.  One method centers around transmission of content and the other is concerned with problem-solving.  A teacher who is imparting information directly to students is using the transmission of content method.  Teachers who wish learners to identify problems and think about solutions are employing the problem-solving method.  Very simply, teachers tend to emphasize one or the other of these two methods—although, of course, teachers often use a mixture of both.  Generally speaking, teachers who lecture most of the time favor content transmission and those who emphasize student needs and interests as the source from which problems arise favor a problem-solving method.

If the term method can be divided into transmission and problem-solving two very large categories, what then is meant by teaching technique?  In popular language, method and technique are often thought of as synonomous.  We reject this usage for it blurs important distinctions.  The overall philosophical approach of teachers—the way they organize themselves to reach important goals—is what we mean by method.  The teacher's specific choice of means to reach this task is technique.  Teachers who organize themselves to present a set of specific skills, attitudes or beliefs naturally wish to enhance this method.  To do so, they may select lectures, 16mm movies, filmstrips or whatever.  However, teachers who wish to improve their students' ability to identify problems, formulate hypotheses, evaluate data, etc., may well select techniques designed to facilitate this end.  Thus, their choice of, say, oral reports, simulations, games, discussion and the like are designed to enhance this goal.  Method, then, refers to the overall aim, goal or approach to teaching; technique is concerned with ways of reaching a goal.

*This chapter was originally published in Methods of Instruction in Social Studies Education, by James L. Barth. (Washington, D.C.: University Press of America, 1979).  It has been revised for the purposes of this text.

Increasingly teachers talk about "strategies." How does strategy fit into method and technique? Very simply, strategies refer to particular ways of organizing a given selection of techniques. For example, if one were to select such teaching techniques as grouping, debates, or quizdowns, these techniques would be coordinated as a strategy. To summarize, then: method refers to one's purpose in teaching a given content. Teaching techniques are the specific means by which one's method, one's general objectives, are reached. And a strategy is simply the way that techniques are organized to accomplish one's objective.

In this chapter, we will examine the rationale for active learning (active vs. passive) and goals towards which active learning has traditionally been aimed. Having examined goals, we turn to a list of 140 teaching techniques and finally examine seven of those techniques in depth.

## Active vs. Passive

Virtually all educational psychologists agree to the proposition that students learn better—learn faster, remember more and derive greater enjoyment—when they are actively involved in learning. It follows that passive students quickly forget what they learn, are bored and resist being prodded to learn anything in the first place. It is for this reason that methods instructors begin with the assumption that methods, techniques and stratevies should emphasize active rather than passive learning.

Well, this is hardly new. I suspect you already knew that persons actively involved in what they are doing are more likely to learn than someone who is not involved. So what's new? The new thought is that all students in class are not actively involved with each technique. Suppose you use the technique of organizing your class into small groups. Out of a class of thirty, twenty might actively participate while ten may be passive about the grouping. At any given moment, during a lecture, only ten percent of the class is listening. When you lecture expect at any given moment only three out of a class of thirty to be "actively" paying attention. Your students are tuning on and off to the lecture from moment to moment so that you can never be quite sure which student actually heard what you were saying. Obviously, one technique to keep active attention with lecture is to require the taking of notes.

The point is that you will need to use a variety of techniques in the hope of getting and keeping the students' attention. In a fifty-five minute period an average of <u>three</u> <u>different</u> techniques are needed to keep active attention. One last thought, students are not equally attracted to each technique. Some respond to debate, while others would hate to debate. Some enjoy and actively watch movies, some sleep (are passive) through movies. Five or six students might actively participate in class discussion, while twenty-five sit silent and passive. Use a variety of techniques because you really don't know what technique will reach which students getting them actively involved on any given day. If you only use one technique, then be prepared to reach actively only a small number of students. A variety of techniques will increase your chance of reaching a greater number of students. It is for this reason that methods teachers say identify a method and a variety of techniques which you plan as a strategy to actively involve all your students.

It is not our desire to tell you exactly what techniques you must employ. This is your decision, based upon your professional expertise. We do join the profession in insisting that whatever techniques you select should emphasize active learning. Please be aware that any given technique, or any set of techniques organized as a strategy, may be either active or passive. A lecture may be passive or active, depending upon student involvement in the process. Grouping may be quite passive. A student oral presentation can be passive. Or all can be active--including lecture-- depending, once more upon whether students are actively involved, committed, and absorbed in what is going on around them.

It is not necessarily the case that social studies is inherently more actively or passively taught than any other subject area. But it does seem as if students, most of whom are required to take social studies, complain about the dullness of the subject. When asked, many students will express dissatisfaction with the boredom attached to wading through a textbook or taking notes on a lecture. The key, then, is to enlist students' active involvement.

Let us examine one specific example. A geography teacher whose instruction is largely passive might ask, "George, what is the capital of Nigeria?" To which George answers, correctly, "Lagos." The teacher's response is,

"Yes, that's right. Lagos is the capital of Nigeria." An active teacher would more likely pose the same question as "George, I wonder why Lagos is the capital of Nigeria and not Kaduna or even Ibadan? Both of these cities seem to be more centrally located." The answer to this question must begin with a central thought—exactly what determines what city will become the "capital" of a given country? Using this as a starting place, students can, with teacher assistance and probing questions, reach their own conclusions as to what characteristics—if any—are necessary for a capital city. The passive, "George, what is the capital of Nigeria," calls for a memorized response, perhaps the lowest form of intellectual activity. The active question requires George to apply, analyze, and evaluate information, and in the end will involve the entire class so that each student will be involved by the question.

In summary, methods, techniques and strategies are important ways of translating goals of education from theory to practice in the classroom. Need we say, as a final comment, to become a professional, as a teacher you must know about the different methods, techniques and strategies.

What I have just said may sound so obvious that you think the point "goes without saying." Well, think again, for if my experience with teachers is any measure the point that a professional teacher ought to know a variety of methods and techniques is in need of repeating. You should want to question the above assertion, surely practicing classroom teachers know not only the difference between methods and techniques but also know and can apply a variety of different techniques. Why not test that assertion out. In your next field experience in the schools ask selected teachers to name for you a variety of different methods and techniques. Then judge for yourself if the point should "go without saying."

A CHART

ILLUSTRATING THE RELATIONSHIP BETWEEN

PLANNING GOALS, METHODS, TECHNIQUES AND STRATEGIES

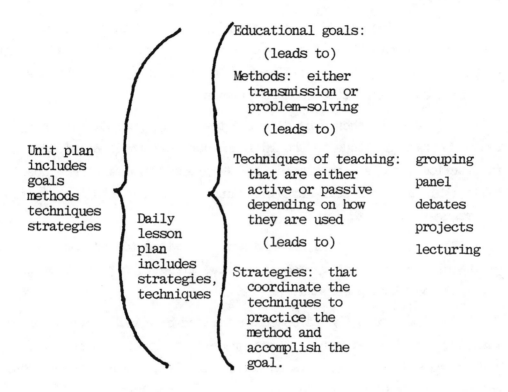

## Working Toward Goals

Any method, any technique or any collection of strategies without goals leads to aimless exercises. You need goals. What is a goal? "All children should be educated to their greatest potential." That's a goal. How about this, "In my class each student will be treated individually accoring to his/her needs and interests." That's also a goal. Goals are ideas and ideals about how you are going to act. They are the things you say to your students, parents, principals and the person who interviewed you for a job. Goals are useful, particularly if they can be realized and if you can use them to guide the application of your knowledge, skills and attitude.

In this text I have identified eight educational goals which, generally speaking, have controlled educators' thinking about how to educate children over the past fifty years. When you read the goals, your first reaction is

liable to be, so what else is new! There is nothing new here, I have heard
it all before. Yes, you have, for when educators speak, out comes the
following goals:

(1)  Teaching should be characterized by efforts to determine
where the students is at the onset of instruction.  Specifically, this
requires diagnosis of his attainment and his problems and the basing
of subsequent instruction on this diagnosis.

(2)  Learning should be directed toward the goal of "learning to
learn."  That is, students should learn not only the content of
instruction but also the generalizeable process of learning.  Specifically, this requires self-sustaining inquiry rather than memorization
and regurgitation of facts.

(3)  Inquiry, in turn, should not be limited to the confines
of the classroom.  Inquiry should involve direct observation of both
physical and human phenomena.

(4)  Classrooms should be characterized by a wide variety of
learning materials--records, tapes, models, programmed materials, filmstrips, pamphlets and television.  Contrarywise, the classroom should
not be dominated by an exclusive reliance on textbooks.

(5)  Teachers should pay attention to and plan around individual
differences.  This implies that there will be a selection of materials
for different reading levels, interests and abilities.  It also implies
that concern for individual differences guides not only use of materials
but grouping, selection of techniques and evaluation.

(6)  Teachers should understand and make conscious use of such
learning principles as reinforcement, motivation and transfer of
training.

(7)  Visitors should see vigorous, even emotionally heated discussions which involve both the entire class and small groups.

(8)  One should find flexible school environments, without substantial concern for grade levels.  There should be extensive use
of team teaching involving groups of teams of teachers, older pupils,
parents and resource persons.

## What Do We Really Know About Learning

The "eight" goals are statements about what authorities in the field say one should ideally experience in school, but is there any research backing these goals? Hopefully the goals are not just wishes. Are you ready to ask, what do we really know about learning? To read an educational psychology book one might assume that educators really know "for sure" quite a bit. I do think we know something about learning, but "for sure" it is modest and some would be unkind enough to say, in fact, darn little. What do we know for sure about the factors for improving instruction?

Contemporary researchers such as Rosenshine and Furst reviewed many studies and summarized their finds to make the following points. Students learn best when factors such as the following are present: clarity; enthusiasm, task oriented, indirectness, including questioning rather than lecturing, frequent use of praise and frequent pupil-to-pupil interaction: and finally the use of all four levels of questions, rather than concentrating on only one level ("The Use of Direct Observation to Study Teaching" in R. Travers (ed.), Second Handbook of Research on Teaching. Chicago: Rand McNally, 1973). Do these factors conflict with any of the ideal goals? No, in fact, they support the goals. So what should you conclude—the goals are, in part, supported by research, but, in part, are the product of wishful thinking.

I do not suggest that the eight goals are, in fact, now being practiced in most schools. They are goals upon which education courses are built and they do represent the ideals toward which many teachers are working, but they are not goals that have been accomplished. To help you think about how you feel about these goals, I have placed them in a chart.

## EDUCATIONAL GOALS

Instructions: Did you ever experience any of these goals in your education? I want you to have a chance to think about this question so would
you please read each of the eight goals in the chart, determine if you
experienced the goal in elementary, secondary or university level, then
write elem., sec., or un. in the appropriate column. When you have
finished all eight goals, add up each column the total number of elem.,
of sec., of un.

| Goals I wish to practice: | Circle Yes or No | Standard practice | Practiced by a few teachers not generally accepted | Teachers do not practice |
|---|---|---|---|---|
| 1. Teaching would be characterized by efforts to determine where the student is at the outset of instruction, to diagnose his attainments and problems, and to base subsequent instruction on the results of this diagnosis. | Yes<br><br>No | | | |
| 2. Learning would be directed toward "learning how to learn," toward self-sustaining inquiry rather than the memorization and regurgitation of facts. | Yes<br><br>No | | | |
| 3. This inquiry would carry the student out of confining classrooms and into direct observation of physical and human phenomena. | Yes<br><br>No | | | |
| 4. Classrooms would be characterized by a wide variety of learning materials—records, tapes, models, programmed materials, filmstrips, pamphlets, and television—and would not be dominated by textbooks. | Yes<br><br>No | | | |

| | | | | |
|---|---|---|---|---|
| 5. Attention to and concern for the individual and individual differences would show through clearly in assignments, class discussions, use of materials, grouping practices and evaluation. | Yes<br>No | | | |
| 6. Teachers would understand and use such learning principles as reinforcement, motivation, and transfer or training. | Yes<br>No | | | |
| 7. Visitors would see vigorous, often heated, small and large group discussions, with the teacher in the background rather than the forefront. | Yes<br>No | | | |
| 8. One would find rather flexible school environments—marked by little attention to grade levels—and extensive use of team teaching activities involving groups of teachers, older pupils, parents, and other persons in the teaching-learning process. | Yes<br>No | | | |
| TOTALS | | elem=<br>sec=<br>un= | elem=<br>sec=<br>un= | elem=<br>sec=<br>un= |

## Interpreting Your Responses

Have you checked the chart twice—once to identify how you were taught and then again how you would like to teach? Now, what do the totals and Yes's and No's tell you about your elementary, secondary, and college education? Do you conclude that you are going to teach in the same way you were taught? Would you conclude that your schools have not employed these goals in teaching you? The 'Educational Goals chart which you have just marked has also been marked by several hundred university students. Their composite results based on how they marked the chart follows. How do your marks compare with others?

|  | Standard Practice | Practice by a few teachers, Not generally accepted | Teachers do not practice |
|---|---|---|---|
|  | elem. 60 | elem. 188 | elem. 513 |
| TOTALS | sec. 53 | sec. 301 | sec. 481 |
|  | un. 58 | un. 286 | un. 435 |

What do the totals suggest? The strongest suggestion is that most of the "eight goals" are not standard practice, nor for that matter are they generally practiced in class by teachers, yet strange as it may seem, teachers, as I said above, agree with the goals. What would you be willing to say about a situation where teachers agree with a set of goals but don't practice those goals.

GOALS I WISH TO PRACTICE

| Standard practice when I teach | Do not wish to practice when I teach |
|---|---|
| 1050 | 85 |

If you say to yourself, yes, I would like to practice some of the above goals of teaching, then you probably will face the problem of trying to practice what was not practiced on you. The totals on the "Goals I Wish to Practice" strongly suggest a favorable response toward the eight goals. The goals are ideas which teachers seem to accept but do not often practice in their teaching. Again we have the very interesting situation where teachers believe in one set of goals but practice another. Yes, of course this separation of ideal goals from the reality of actual classroom teaching leads to problems.

<u>Do</u> <u>As</u> <u>I</u> <u>Say</u>

I think it is significant—and the evidence suggests—that teachers tend to follow patterns of teaching that they have experienced in their own education. And they follow their own experience regardless of whether such patterns have been effective. The evidence strongly suggests, just look at the totals above, that teachers are taught throughout their formal education with passive techniques.

May we admit that the old saying "do as I say, not as I do" describes part of our difficulty. Perhaps it is easier now to explain why teachers believe in one set of goals but practice another by knowing that we copy what was done to us. We know how we were taught, we know what people do and, in fact, we have learned not to pay much attention to what people say. So here you are in a methods couse that says, "Do as I say, forget how the university courses have been taught, forget about your elementary and secondary experiences with teachers, try to build a different vision that you have never really known." Well, I am not sure how successful that plea will be, for in fact, all evidence suggests you will do what was done to you.

I point this out not to discourage you or to place teaching in a negative context, but to be truthful and realistic about how your past will probably affect your future performance. To know your past experience with education is to be warned about the decisions you are likely to make in the future. Consider yourself warned.

<u>Teaching</u> <u>Techniques</u>

If you're going to be active rather than passive as a teacher, no matter what level you're teaching, it should be rather obvious by now that there is little alternative than to practice a variety of teaching techniques. As I have said, you will need to select an overall methodology which will govern how you intend to apply the techniques. The techniques you choose will need to be organized, for undoubtedly over a period of time you will use a number of techniques. That organization is called strategy. Both your method and your strategy call for planning. Planning methods, strategies, and techniques are exceedingly important if you wish to accomplish certain specific goals. The remainder of this chapter I will devote to specific teaching techniques. First I will list 140 teaching techniques and from that list select seven rather basic ones which we will look at in some depth.

I could tell you that there are literally hundreds of different teaching techniques. Teachers are often told to use their own imaginations in thinking up different techniques, but often they can't, so they are required to take methods courses in which techniques are emphasized, and of course, there are always long lists of techniques which presumably they will learn. But it has been my experience that many teachers, when asked to recall different techniques, find it difficult to recall more than a few. I won't try to explain that phenomena here, for that was covered above with the "do as I say, not as I do" argument. Suffice to say that teachers generally have limited recall of specific techniques though there are hundreds, perhaps thousands of known techniques.

Suppose I were to say to you right now, imagine you were teaching on the topic of ecology and you were asked to list at least ten different techniques you might use in class to teach about this topic. Can you list ten techniques? It is not unusual for teachers to list no more than perhaps two or three techniques. Secondary teachers are notoriously worse than elementary teachers at identifying techniques. The fact that there are hundreds of techniques really doesn't mean much if in practice only few can be recalled.

## Listing Teaching Techniques

1. Lecture by instructor
2. Class discussion conducted by instructor
3. Recitation: oral questions by instructor answered orally by students
4. Discussion groups conducted by selected student chairpersons
5. Lecture—demonstration by instructor
6. Lecture—demonstration by another instructor(s) from a special field
7. Presentations by a panel of instructors or pupils
8. Presentations by student panels from the class: class invited to participate
9. Student reports given by individuals
10. Student-group reports given by committees from the class
11. Debates on current issues by students from the class (informal)
12. Class discussions conducted by a student or student committee

13. Forums
14. Bulletin boards
15. Busy groups
16. Choral speaking
17. Collecting
18. Textbook assignment
19. Reading assignments in journals, monographs, etc.
20. Reading assignments in supplementary books
21. Assignment to outline portions of textbook
22. Assignment to outline certain supplementary readings
23. Dabates (formal)
24. Crossword puzzles
25. Cooking food of places studied
26. Construction of vocabulary lists
27. Vocabulary drills
28. Diaries
29. Dances of places or periods studied
30. Construction of summaries by students
31. Dressing dolls
32. Required term paper
33. Panels
34. Biographical reports given by students
35. Reports on published research studies and experiments by students
36. Library research on topics or problems
37. Written book reports by students
38. Flags
39. Jigsaw puzzle maps
40. Hall of Fame (females)
41. Flannel boards
42. Use of pre-test
43. Gaming and simulation
44. Flashcards
45. Flowcharts
46. Interviews
47. Maps, transparencies, globes
48. Mobiles

49. Audio-tutorial lesson (individualized instruction)

50. Models

51. Music

52. Field trips

53. Drama

54. Open textbook study

55. Committee projects--small groups

56. Note books

57. Murals and montages

58. Class projects

59. Individual projects

60. Quizdown

61. Modeling in various media

62. Pen pals

63. Photographs

64. Laboratory experiments performed by more than two students working together

65. Use of dramatization, skits, plays

66. Student construction of diagrams, charts, or graphs

67. Making of posters by students

68. Students drawing pictures or cartoons to vividly portray principles or facts

69. Problem-solving or case studies

70. Puppets

71. Use of chalkboard by instructor as an aid in his teaching

72. Use of diagrams, tables, graphs, and charts by instructor in his teaching

73. Use of exhibits and displays by instructor

74. Reproductions

75. Construction of exhibits and displays by students

76. Use of slides

77. Use of filmstrips

78. Use of motion pictures, educational films

79. Use of theater motion pictures

80. Use of recordings

81. Use of radio programs

82. Use of television
83. Role playing
84. Sandtables
85. School affiliations
86. Verbal illustrations:  use of anecdotes and parables to illustrate
87. Service projects
88. Stamps, coins, and other hobbies
89. Use of community or local resources
90. Story-telling
91. Surveys
92. Tutorial:  students assigned to other students for assistance
93. Coaching:  special assistance provided for students having difficulty in the course
94. Oral reports
95. Word association device
96. Workbooks
97. Using case studies reported in the literature to illustrate psychological principles and facts
98. Construction of scrapbooks
99. Applying simple statistical techniques to class data
100. Time lines
101. "Group dynamics" techniques
102. Units of instruction organized by topics
103. Non-directive techniques applied to the classroom
104. Supervised study during class period
105. Use of sociometric text to make sociometric analysis of the class
106. Use of audio-visual materials and equipment
107. Open textbook tests
108. Put idea into a picture
109. Write a caption for chart, picture, cartoon
110. Reading aloud
111. Differentiated assignment and homework
112. Telling about a trip
113. Mock convention
114. Filling out forms (income tax, checks)
115. Prepare editorial for school paper

44

116.  Attend a city council meeting
117.  Exchanging "things"
118.  Making announcements
119.  Taking part (community elections)
120.  Playing music from other countries or times
121.  Studying local history
122.  Compile list of older citizens as resource people
123.  Students from abroad (exchange students)
124.  Obtain free and low cost materials
125.  Collect old magazines (National Geographic, Life)
126.  Collect colored slides
127.  Visit an "ethnic" restaurant
128.  Specialize in one country
129.  Follow a world leader (in the media)
130.  Visit employment agency
131.  Start a campaign
132.  Conduct a series
133.  Investigate a life
134.  Assist an immigrant
135.  Volunteer (tutoring, hospital)
136.  Prepare an exhibit
137.  Detect propaganda
138.  Join an organization
139.  Collect money for a cause
140.  Elect a "Hall of Fame" (males)

## Seven Techniques You Ought to Know

I have identified from the list of 140 techniques seven that I call fundamental, that is, seven techniques which I think are the most likely to offer you a variety of alternatives for teaching social studies. The two most popular techniques which I am sure you have experienced throughout your formal education are lecturing and recitation. In any list of techniques these two will always appear, for they are the two most practiced in class. Though they are not by nature passive techniques, they are so often remembered and used by teachers that through repetition they become passive, and of course, this is true for any technique. A technique used repeatedly can well become passive. Besides the two well-known lecturing and recitation techniques, the seven techniques you ought to recall and apply are: grouping, drama, oral reports, debate, panel, quizdown, and the seventh which is not so much a technique but an application of media to your teaching.

Grouping: Grouping has become one of the most popular techniques. Its popularity has grown over the years because of the increased emphasis upon active student participation. It is difficult for a teacher with a class of thirty to forty students to provide an opportunity for each to participate during each class period. Grouping offers one technique by which students in groups participate among themselves and in so doing become actively involved in the class work. Students reluctant to participate in class recitation can be encouraged to be involved in small group discussions.

The most recent devlopment in grouping has been the identification of at least five different types of groups for instructional purposes. The following five types illustrate the different purposes and guidelines for organizing small groups.

1. Task-Oriented Small Group

   Purpose: to bring the various members of the small group together to focus on a specific project or proposal.

   Guidelines: 1) clearly define your task so that all members understand and agree. 2) Sharply delineate roles and assignments for the individual members of the group.

2. Brainstorming Small Group

   Purpose: to bring the various member of the small group together to discuss freely and uninhibitedly a topic which is problem centered or solution centered.

   Guidelines: 1) The ideal number for a "Brainstorming" group is about twelve. 2) The topic should be relatively simple, familiar and talkable. 3) Criticism is ruled out; judgment of ideas is done at a later time. 4) Quantity of participation is wanted.

3. Tutorial Small Group

   Purpose: to emphasize individual instruction usually of a remedial nature or to evaluate an independent study project of an advance nature.

   Guidelines: 1) Remedial work should be of a type that is general enough to benefit all members of a small group. 2) The emphasis is on the teacher dealing with each member of the group in turn.  3) No attempt is made here for group dynamics and interaction between students.

4. <u>Discursive</u> Small Group

Purpose:  to encourage free and uninhibited discussion by students of a topic which has some previous structure and relevance to material under consideration.

Guidelines:  1) Structure of topic should be presented to students prior to their coming to seminar.  2) The teacher acts primarily as an interested observer—listens attentively, notices who participates, watches for student reaction.

5. <u>Socratic</u> Small Group

Purpose:  to bring students and instructors together to discuss a problem posed by the teacher for which an answer can best be determined through the open and honest exchange of informed opinion.

Guidelines:  1) Begins in Stage 1, with teacher challenging, disturbing, demanding definitions, driving the discussants back into a corner to examine their prejudices, to defend their positions.  2) During the second stage the teacher does a lot of good hard listening; then becomes a leader and participant—probing, directing, stimulating, enticing, responding, challenging, and synthesizing.

<u>Drama</u>:  The technique of drama involves the student in a dramatization (role-playing) of some event or feeling.  The drama is one way of encouraging students to learn through dramatization, by expressing in their own words the drama of the event.  Some authorities will classify drama under the heading of role-playing, and of course, much of what happens in drama is role-playing.  Many teachers have begun to take role-playing seriously because it does force students to be actively involved in a situation.  The dramatization provides an active situation in which the student not only participates but often interprets.  Normally drama is used in one of three ways in the classroom:  psychodrama, extemporaneous, formal written drama.

Some teachers use psychodrama to help students express their fears and anxieties.  The use of this particular technique should be limited to those who have been trained in the use of psychodrama techniques.

Many teachers  use an extemporaneous form of drama.  This form emphasizes the student responding to a situation or a set of feelings without prior preparation. The teacher might ask students to dramatize an historical situation such as George Washington crossing the Deleware River on Christmas Eve. The crew of the boat asks him questions. What might Columbus have said to the natives when he stepped ashore? How might the African slaves have felt when they were loaded on ships for transport to the American continent? What might their thoughts have been? Did they experience pain? Possibly the class can act out the answers to these questions.

Teachers have also used a formal written drama or play to put emphasis upon certain historical events. The play is often written by the students and acted for the class or classes.

Oral Reports: One of the favorite techniques among experienced teachers is oral reports. Normally this technique requires a student to report to the class on a particular topic. Teachers have traditionally favored this technique because it has placed emphasis upon research and oral presentation both of which are thought to be important skills. The oral report can be informal such as when the student is asked to report on some personal incident he may have knowledge of, or formal as when the student is required to research a topic.

The fact that oral reporting is a favorite technique also suggests that as a technique it is often abused. The obvious intention of the teacher is to encourage the student to have something to say (through research, personal experience, or reporting results) and thus practice the skill of communicating this to the class. The oral report tends to break down when there is no criteria for a good presentation. The practice has been for teachers to concentrate on research techniques and other means of gathering information, but have not offered equal standards for oral presentation. Keep in mind that oral reporting as a technique can be very effective if there is criteria by which the student and the teacher can judge the quality of the presentation.

Debate: Debate as a classroom technique, is normally used by teachers to encourage students to apply the knowledge they have acquired. It is also used to help students develop the skill of preparing arguments for one or another side of an issue. Debate is used in either a formal or informal way. Some teachers like to require their students to learn formal rules of debate. The intent is to teach students the procedures for developing formal argumentation. Most teachers, however, use debate in an informal way, that is without the formal rules of debate. The informal technique is intended to prepare students to defend a particular point of view. The informal technique permits the teacher and students to develop their own set of rules by which the class will debate. It is intended that the students be actively involved in preparing and defending positions. Teachers often use this technique to teach students that there are not only different points of view but that positions are debatable.

Panel Discussions: Teachers use panel discussions to present information to the class. The panel often consists of a number of students who are assigned to a particular topic. Normally the panel orally reports their findings to the class on the assigned topic. Some teachers also require that the report be written as well as orally reported. The panel differs from debate in that it is not intended as a means for stimulating debate among the panel members but rather as a systematic way for a group of students to present their research findings.

Quizdowns: Quizdowns are used primarily to involve students in the recall of information. Some teachers use the quizdown as a technique for reviewing before a test, some use it as a technique for evaluating, and others have used it as a game to stimulate team spirit in a class. As a review technique it is intended to stimulate students to quickly respond to a set of review questions which the teacher has prepared. In some quizdowns the students are asked to stand either along the side of the room or beside their desks. When they fail to correctly answer the question, they are required to sit down. The students or students who remain standing at the end of the review are referred to as the winners. Some teachers use this technique as a means of evaluating the progress of the class in learning certain specific events. Some teachers have successfully used this technique as a game. Students in the class are teamed so that teams compete against each other rather than individuals. The team that answers the most questions correctly is considered the winner. This technique stimulates participation and strengthens the students' enthusiasm for learning, if not for personal satisfaction then for the welfare of the team.

Extending Yourself Through Media: We have said up to this point that as alternatives to lecturing and recitation which includes question and answer and discussion techniques you ought to think of grouping, drama, oral reports, debate, panel, and quizdowns. These, if properly applied as active learning techniques, should help you be a more effective teacher by involving students through participation. Active learning through participation may help your students learn, but beyond that one additional way to be effective is through the use of media. Often it is not enough to provide your students with debates, reports, groupings; it is equally important to provide them with sights and sounds. The use of media in social studies is particularly important because much of the content deals with abstractions, i.e., democracy, freedom, manifest destiny. It is important to illustrate past history, it is important to demonstrate ideas, it important to provide models. We need not belabor this argument for few teachers would argue that illustration is not a significant part of teaching and that those illustrations that most clearly transmit a clear picture are the most effective. Media is a means, a technique by which you extend your thinking to others. A loudspeaker extends your voice, a blackboard you have written on is an extension of your thinking, a tape recorder is an extension of your voice, an opaque projector is an extended projection of your ideas written large. A movie is an illustration of ideas you have, slides are specific illustrations of ideas which you wish your students to see. In summary, audio-visual equipment—whether tape recorders, public address system, movies, slides, or overhead projector with transpariencies—are merely means by which you extend yourself. By ourselves we are limited in the reach of our voice and in our ability to verbally illustrate meaning. Media provides us with the capability of enlarging our capacity to reach others.

## Criteria for Using Active Learning Techniques

Each of the seven techniques we have listed above will require you to plan for their proper application to your classroom. Before planning to use these techniques you should consider the following questions. These questions, of course, provide a criteria which should guide your application.

A. Of what value is this activity to your students? For example, is this activity intended to increase their skills, their knowledge, their thinking ability?

B. What specific procedures have you developed for carrying out this activity?  For example, what rules have you set up for debate?  What procedures have you announced for holding an effective panel discussion?  What rules have you set up for oral reports?

C.  Can you identify common mistakes which you should watch out for in applying the technique?  For example, a common mistake with grouping is that the groups are not sure of what they are supposed to do.  Another common mistake is that students are not provided limits on their oral reports, and quizdowns do not fulfill their promise if the questioning is not kept at a fast pace.

D.  What criteria have you developed for evaluating the students' performance?  If you are to evaluate the students' performance in any of these activities, you must develop a clear set of criteria that both you and the students understand.  What are the ingredients of a good oral report?  By what criteria are you going to evaluate a panel discussion?  How will you know that a grouping is successful?  How will you evaluate the quality of a drama?

Giving and Getting Information

Would you think with me about giving and getting information.  Some teaching techniques are useful to give information and some are useful to get.  I want you to think about give and get from a teacher's point of view.  Generally, when a teacher applies a technique, it is either to give or get something from students.  Lecture is give.  Panel is get.  Quizdowns to give information.  Recitation is getting information from students, whereas grouping (task-oriented, brainstorming, discursive, socratic) are intended to get.  Tutorial, small group could be used either way.  Drama (role-playing) is intended to get as is a question and answer session.  Finally, oral reports would be what—give or get information from the student?  Did you answer "get", for that is usually the teacher's purpose for using the technique.

By now you're thinking—a technique is either give or get depending on how the technique is used.  Right, so if you were to say from the student's point of view an oral report is giving information, you would be right, but from a teacher's point of view the technique is intended to get student to get information and report it orally.

Techniques from the teacher's point of view can be thought of this way:

| Techniques to give information | Techniques to get information |
|---|---|
| lecture | recitation and |
| media (filmstripts, | discussion |
| slides, movies) | small groups |
| field trips | drama (role-playing) |
| individualized | debates |
| instruction | quizdowns |
| | oral reports |
| | panel |

Inspection of the list above suggests that most techniques are intended to get students to respond. Now try your understanding. Would you turn back, right now, to the list of 140 techniques and quickly look down the list starting with number one. "Lecture by instructor" and mentally say to yourself: "As a teacher I would use this technique to either <u>give</u> or <u>get</u> information from my students."

Probably all 140 techniques can be classified giving or getting, or perhaps some are both. So what, is there a point to all this? The point is that the exclusive use of either give or get can lead to passive learning. Teachers who use only techniques that get information: questioning, panels, debates, term papers and projects run the risk of having student perceive their class as monotonous (doing the same old thing). From the teacher's point of view many techniques were used, from the students' point of view the activities have all been getting from the students. Getting techniques may leave students believing they are doing all the work--though as teachers we know they are not.

<u>Warning</u>: <u>Active</u> <u>Learning</u> <u>Requires</u> <u>Student</u> <u>Skills</u>

Many experienced teachers don't use a variety of teaching techniques. Teachers will say, "I tried that technique many years ago and it doesn't work with these students." What teachers discovered as they tried the techniques is that students didn't have the skills necessary to make the technique work. Grouping, debates, panels don't normally work unless students have reading, research and oral presentation skills. Elementary teachers expect to develop the students' skills, but this is not equally true of secondary teachers who have much more of a commitment to the

academic discipline. If, as a teacher, your interest is rooted in covering historical events and you can find no time to develop the skills of
reading, comprehension, oral communication, writing and researching, then
you ought not to use active learning techniques because they probably will
not work for you and your students. If, on the other hand, you develop
a plan throughout the semester to improve your students' oral, written, and
research skills, then you students will be prepared to participate in active
learning. Realize that the successful practice of teaching techniques
requires certain levels of student skill development. If the technique
doesn't work it probably means the students are not sufficiently skilled.
Don't abandon the technique but develop the skill.

## Summary Conclusion

I have attempted in this chapter to distinguish between methods, techniques, and strategies, to provide a rationale for active teaching as
opposed to passive  teaching, and finally to identify seven specific techniques from among 140. I have pointed out that there are perhaps only
two real methods (transmission and problem-solving) but an infinite number
of teaching techniques. A strategy is merely the plan by which the techniques are coordinated to accomplish the method. Educators are almost
unanimous in their recommendation that teachers use active learning techniques with, of course, the hope that by encouraging students to participate they will be more effective learners. Finally you were asked to
identify seven basic techniques:  grouping, oral reports, drama, panel,
quizdown, debate, and use of media. When you sit down to plan your class
lessons, I hope you will never be at a loss to recall at least the basic
techniques. Being a professional means that you know things that the non-
professional does not know. Remember your methods and techniques for they
are part of what will establish you as a professional teacher. Oh, by the
way, can you recall five types of grouping and seven techniques of teaching?

PART II:   UNIT 4

THE TRANSMISSION METHOD OF INSTRUCTION

Larry D. Wills

In Unit 4 and the next Unit 5, you will be introduced to two differing methods of instruction:   transmission and problem-solving.   Each method is designed to achieve differing objectives and reflects differing theories of learning.   For purposes of this chapter, we will first discuss why one would choose the transmission method and then present a step-by-step outline of how you might construct a transmission lesson.

A lesson or unit designed around the transmission method has as its main purpose to explain, to set forth, content which you want your students to learn.   Notice the word "you," meaning the teacher, was underlined.   In a transmission lesson the teacher decides the mode and pace of instruction.   The student is the listener and is quite passive in terms of what is to be learned. The goal is for the students to possess a body of knowledge specified by the teacher and be able to apply those facts and concepts to new situations or problems which are new to the students.   The teacher's responsibility is to carefully plan each learning activity so that students can achieve that goal. The students are not required to be beyond the material which has been pre-sented or to make independent decisions.

They fear this method of instruction leads only to rote memorization and is a principal cause of boredom in the classroom.   Such a criticism does not have to apply.   An important objective of any social studies classroom should be for students to master a body of concepts or generalizations found among the various social sciences.   Meaningful verbal learning can be an important objective for your students.

For the lesson using the transmission method, your first task is to identify those facts, concepts, and generalizations you think are important for that particular lesson or unit.   You may want to refer at this time to Part II, Unit 1 for a review of facts, concepts, and generalizations.

For our purposes, assume you want your students to understand that all people in social groups play certain roles.   A role is the behavior expected of a person because of his position in the social structure or group.   You also want the students to understand that roles are like a coin with two sides:  all roles have both rights and status.  A <u>right</u> is an opportunity for someone to act verbally or physically; one's <u>status</u> is that which one achieves having played such a role.  These are the main ideas you want to put across to your students in the lesson.

Now you are ready to state your behavioral objectives.  They might look like the following:

1.  The student should be able to define role, rights, and status;

2.  Given the classroom with roles of student and teacher, the student should be able to give examples of rights and responsibilities held by the role of teacher and student; and

3.  Given a social group chosen by the student, the student should be able to apply the concepts of rights and status by providing specific examples of each.

For objective one, the teacher will be responsible for providing an explanation of the concepts role, rights, and responsibilities.  This might be achieved by students reading from the text, a short monologue given by the teacher on meanings of the terms with assistance of visual aids, films, tapes, etc.  For objective number two, the teacher again has the responsibility for "leading" or guiding the students through an application of the concepts to a social group common to all—the classroom.  Following the reading or explanation, the following dialogue might take place.  I would like you now to open your notebooks and write your definition in your own words, of role, rights, and status.  See if you can use words which were not part of the reading.  Here the teacher should spotcheck some of the written answers by asking students to recite.

Teacher:  Now that we have defined what is meant by role, rights, and status, let's see how we can apply these terms to our own classroom.  First of all, we have learned that my role of teacher includes all those things which you, the principal, your parents, and I feel I should do as a teacher.  On the chalkboard, let's list some of the things we can think of that make up my role; . . . these are my rights or what I am expected to do.  Well, for one thing, I am expected to take attendance and make certain there is some order and discipline in the classroom.  Can anyone think of other rights which I have?

Mary:       "You are expected to teach us—that is your responsibility and why you get paid."

Teacher:    "Yes, I am expected to prepare lessons, and try to make them as interesting as possible."

Jody:       "Yeah, and you are also expected to give us a grade—which I wish some time you would forget to do."

Teacher:    "Now, Jody, what would happen if I did not turn in grade cards at the end of the six weeks grading period?"

Jody:       "Well, I suppose the principal would get mad and some of the other teachers would think you were not meeting your responsibility."

Teacher:    "That's right. So in order for me to perform my role as teacher and do those things that are within my understood right, there are certain things I get in return, such as getting paid. That which I get for performing my rights is a kind of status. Now that we have listed some of my rights in the classroom, let's now list some of the things which I get for performing those rights. We will call these items "status." One status item I receive is attention when I am teaching class. When I begin to talk, you are supposed to listen. That is a kind of status. I have also talked to many of your parents, and they seem to respect me as a teacher, and even some of you have come up and said that you like me as a teacher. That is a kind of status. All of these things I receive for performing my role as teacher. Now let us look at your role as a student. We will do the same as we did for teacher by listing your rights and your status items."

At this point, the teacher continues the lesson using the same concepts but with different examples. He works with the students, guiding them with examples to understand the concepts of the lesson.

Toward the end of the lesson after the teacher has listed rights and status elements of the student's role in the classroom, the teacher should review the definition of the concepts and check to see if there are any questions before going into the assignment for the next day.

To this point, the teacher has guided student responses and discussion of subject matter. The teacher has been very much in control and student answers have been related to content under discussion. "Good" transmission teaching does not stop here, however. In order to evaluate whether students consider classroom discussion, the next step is to see whether the students can apply those concepts to a problem situation not studied before. For our purposes, the teacher might ask the students to choose a social group, such as the family or church, and go through the same process as done in class. In this way the student would be required to analyze a social group and apply the concepts of the lesson.

Now let's review some of the important steps you should include in a lesson or unit built around the transmission method.

1. The teacher should have well-formulated objectives in mind before presentation of lesson.

2. The lesson should be sequential in nature, going from the known to the unknown.

3. The lesson should actively involve the students in the learning process, requiring them to apply concepts and generalization to some problem identified by the teacher.

PART TWO:   UNIT FIVE

THE PROBLEM-SOLVING METHOD OF INSTRUCTION

SHEILA A. WINEMAN

In Unit 4, Wills introduced the transmission method of instruction.  A
review of this chapter will point to the fact that the transmission method is
a teacher-oriented method in that the teacher identifies the specific content
to be mastered, chooses the mode and pace of instruction, and directs the students
in applying the newly-learned concepts to new and different situations.  Further
analysis of the transmission method should lead to the conclusion that there are
definitely times when it is appropriate for use in the social studies classroom.

Another method of instruction which should receive "equal time" in the
social studies is problem-solving.  Unlike the transmission method, problem-solving
can be viewed as a student-oriented method, since there is an attempt to provide
first-hand problem experiences which encourage students to make inquiries and
discover concepts for themselves.  Through such experiences, children can develop
basic problem-solving skills which will serve them well as they inquire into
problem situations in all phases of their lives.  Because the development of
independent problem-solvers is a goal for education in general and social studies
in particular, the use of this method should definitely be considered.

As noted above, the development of independent problem-solvers can be
achieved through the problem-solving method.  However, the amount of teacher
direction provided and the complexity of the problems presented must be carefully
regulated in order for this development to occur.  Simple problems which provide
fairly structured directions should be provided for children who are taking part
in problem-solving experiences for the first time.  As they become more comfortable
with this approach to learning, more complex problems can be used and less teacher
direction will be needed.

When simple problem-solving activities are used, the teacher presents a
problem related to the topic being studied, provides specific directions as to
how the students can inquire into the problem, and suggests at least one creative
way to share discoveries.  For example, if the problems and needs of senior citizens
is the topic being explored, a possible problem-solving activity might be the
following:

The government needs your help! You have been contacted by the President's Council on Aging to help make the general public more aware of Grandparent's Day, a new holiday.

1. Discuss these questions with a friend:

   a. What's special about grandparents?
      What do they do to help us?
      What can we learn from them?

   b. What special needs and problems do grandparents have? What can we do to help them?

   c. How can we remind the general public about some of these things?

2. Find out all you can about Grandparent's Day. The articles and pictures in the learning center will help you.

   Find at least three important facts you could present to the public about this holiday.

3. Choose at least one of the following projects to share your discoveries:

   a. Design and draw a mini-billboard about Grandparent's Day. Be sure to use some of the information you discovered in the articles or in your discussion with a friend.

      Display your billboard on the learning center bulletin board.

   b. Design a bumper sticker to remind people of Grandparent's Day or to remind people that grandparents are special.

      Display your bumper sticker on the learning center bulletin board.

c.   Prepare a radio broadcast to announce Grandparent's Day and remind people that grandparents are special. Share your broadcast with the class on Discovery Day. (You might like to make your broadcast to the entire school by using the intercom. Check with the teacher for details!)

In this simple problem-solving activity, the problem is clearly defined and the directions for inquiring into the problem are explicit. The students are asked to explore their own thoughts and ideas, along with some article information, in order to make discoverieson their own. The students can choose from among several alternatives in sharing their discoveries, but their choices must be one of those listed by the teacher. For some students, such activities may be a helpful stepping stone from past experiences, which were almost totally teacher-directed, to more self-directed problem-solving experiences.

Keeping in mind the earlier description of the problem-solving method and the need to provide simple activities for inexperienced students, consider the following general guidelines for problem-solving activities:

1. Whenever possible, problem-solving activities should emphasize active rather than passive learning. "Passive learning" requires the student to simply be a receiver of information. The student who listens to a teacher tell about the Boston Tea Party and explain why it happened is involved in passive learning. "Active learning," on the other hand, requires the student to be a developer of information. An example of this would be a student who "becomes" a drummer boy with the American troops during the Battle of Bunker Hill and writes a letter to his parents telling them what happened. This student would make inquiries into the "problems" encountered by the drummer boy, discover some answers, and interpret these discoveries through his written letter. Thus, the student has developed his own information and understandings through active involvement.

2. All problem-solving activities should contain three elements. These three-elements are:

   A. Present the problem.
   B. Provide questions and directions.
   C. Provide a creative way to share the discoveries.

The following sample problem-solving activity identifies the three elements:

1. Think of the rules you have in your home.

(PROBLEM) 2. Pretend that for one week there are no rules! <u>Everyone</u> in the family can do just what he/she wants to do!

(DIRECTIONS) 3. Think about these questions:

(QUESTIONS)

    a. What would that week be like?
    b. What rules would you enjoy breaking? Why?
    c. Would you like to live all the time without any rules in your home? Why, or why not?

(DIRECTIONS) 4. Write your answers to the questions in #3 in your Personal Progress File.

(DIRECTIONS) 5. Choose one of the following ways to show what you think the week would be like:

    a. Write a story about the week without rules. Add a sentence at the end telling whether you feel rules are important and why.

    b. Draw a picture showing something about the week without rules. Write a caption for the picture that tells whether you feel rules are needed.

    c. Role-lay what might happen during the week without rules. End the role-play with a statement telling whether you feel rules are needed.

(DIRECTIONS) 6. Be ready to share all your discoveries at the next Sharing Session.

The problem presented in the example above is a fairly simplistic one. The child uses guiding questions to help him make internal inquiries (review his personal knowledge and experience in relation to the problem) about rules he has at home and what life would be like without these rules. He's then asked to choose one of three creative ways to share his discoveries about the need for these rules.

Problem-solving activities developed on various social studies topics might require both internal and external inquiry (analyzing sources outside oneself for information). The external inquiry might be anything from polling the neighborhood to find out how many different groups to which family members belong, to using text books, library books, and other resources to find out about the various festivals held in Alaska. Regardless of the type of inquiry used, <u>the child will be actively involved in solving a problem.</u>

The creative sharing adds another element of active involvement to the problem-solving activity. It also gives the child an opportunity to summarize his findings for the teacher and the other students.

NOTE: A helpful list of experiences which may be used for creative sharing can be found in Unit 10, page 118.

3.  When the problem-solving method is used, the teacher has choices as to how the actual problem is presented to the students. The teacher may present the problem orally to the entire class, allow the children to inquire on their own, and then call them back together as a group to share and discuss their discoveries. Another approach would be to divide the class into small groups, give each group a problem-solving activity (presented to the group either orally or in written form--each group receiving the same activity or a different activity for each group), allow time for inquiries and discoveries, and have each group share their discoveries. A third option would be to provide problem-solving experiences on cards or folders (or tape record the activities for non-readers) and place them in a learning center to be used independently by the students. A Sharing Session would be held after all the children have experienced the activities.

4.  Principles or "big ideas" represent the foundation for the development of P.S. activities. Any topic in social studies (whether it be a unit on the community from an elementary social studies textbook or a student-initiated study of family roots) is built upon certain key principles or big ideas. When P.S. activites are developed in such an area of study, the teacher's goal is to design activities which will enable a student to discover the meaning of these big ideas for himself. For example, a big idea associated with the study of homes around the world might be: People meet their fundamental needs in various ways. Therefore, the teacher would design a P.S. activity (or activities) which would guide a student to the discovery of this big idea and its meaning. Such an activity might be similar to the following example:

HOMES & FAMILIES - #1

1.  Look at the house in this picture.

2.  Compare the house with your house. How are they alike? How are they different? Why are they different?

3.  Write your answers on the chart in your social studies folder.

4.  Which house would you rather live in? Why?

5.  Who do you think lives in the house in the picture?

6.  Write a story about the house and the people who live in it. Pin your story to the Social Studies Fact Line.

7.  Tell your story to a group at the Sharing Session.

(If you would care to know how the people in Northern Canada sometimes build their homes, read pages 87-91 of The Adventures of Oolakuk.)

Materials:  picture of Eskimo family, home in Norther Canada; companion chart

5.  In some cases, information beyond what the child discovers may be provided for further clarification of the big idea. Examine the preceding P.S. activity again. The child will probably make internal inquiries (review his personal knowledge in relation to the topic) and external inquiries (check available resources for information) related to this activity which will result in the discovery of the big idea. However, he may want further evidence that his efforts have led to an appropriate conclusion. Therefore, additional information (i.e., a book which gives an explanation and pictures of how "ice homes" are built) may be provided. Alternative techniques for providing additional information or clarification might be:

> If you wold care to know more about how people in Northern Canada sometimes build their homes:
>
>> -look on the index card in the envelope on the back of this folder.
>>
>> -look at the filmstrip in the viewer.
>>
>> -look on page 41 of the C encyclopedia.
>>
>> -listen to the cassette tape on your table.

---

Ruttan, Robert A.  The Adventures of Oolakuk.  Englewood Cliffs:  Prentice-Hall, 1969.

"If you would care to know" should precede the directions for obtaining additional information. If the child cares to know, the information should be available. On the other hand, insisting that a disinterested child listen to a tape or look in a book may result in negative feelings toward that subject.

6.  <u>Problem-solving activities should be easily understood by the students.</u> If a child is to learn to solve problems independently, he must be able to understand the problem presented to him! If reading the activity causes difficulty, an alternative would be to record it on a cassette tape. On the other hand, when problem-solving activities are written on cards or folders for independent use by the students, they should be written in simple language. Short, clear directions that tell the child exactly what to do, how to do it, and what to do with the end-product should be included. Examples can sometimes be helpful, such as giving the child a chart form to use if the activity asks him to make a chart, or providing a sample graph if the activity asks him to graph some type of information. If the activity is lengthy, separating it into smaller segments on the card or folder can make it easier to read and understand. Numbering each direction in the activity can also add clarity. Pictures and drawings add color and interest, as well as contributing to the clarity of the activity.

7.  <u>A well-developed problem-solving activity calls for more than a simple "yes" or "no" response.</u> Consider these concluding questions from an activity:

Is there a difference in the 1973 and 1983 price lists you made?

Do you think meat prices have risen since 1973?

The first question provides a "clue" to what will happen when the student performs the activity and the final question asks the student to simply recall what he's done. Be re-writing these final questions, the "clue" can be eliminated and the student can be asked to do more than demonstrate his recall ability.

Example:      Is there a difference in the 1973 and 1983
              price lists?

              Do you think prices have risen since 1970?

Re-Written:   Examine the two price lists you have made.

              How are they alike?  How are they different?

              Record your answers.

Use the form in the folder to make a chart showing your
discoveries.

No clues are provided in the re-written example, and the child
is asked to practice the problem-solving skills of observation,
description, interpretation, and communication.

8.  <u>Open-ended questions occur frequently in well-developed P.S.
    activities</u>.  "Open-ended" refers to questions which call for
    creative, imaginative responses.  There may be questions such as
    the following:

    How could you solve this problem?

    How could you test your hypotheis?

    Open-ended questions often begin with words or phrases such as
    those given below:

        Compare...

        Explain...

        Predict...

        Create...

        Develop...

        What do you suppose would happen if...

        Try to develop a new way of..........

        What would you do if.................

        Suppose you were to..................

        How many ways can you think of to.....

        How could you test your ideas about...

9. <u>Problem-solving activities should be designed to strengthen problem-solving skills</u>. Carefully developed problem-solving activities should provide many opportunities for practicing the problem-solving skills listed below:

|                |                |
|----------------|----------------|
| observation    | analysis       |
| classification | description    |
| interpretation | inference      |
| deduction      | hypothesizing  |
| predicting     | planning       |
| experimentation| measurement    |
| communication  | generalization |

NOTE: For a defintion of each of the problem-solving skills, see Unit 9, page 106.

Refer again to the sample problem-solving activity related to rules in the home given earlier in this unit. In that activity, the child would be <u>analyzing</u> the rules in his home; <u>hypothesizing</u> as to what a week without rules would be like; <u>analyzing</u>, <u>inferring</u>, and <u>communicating</u> as he responds to the questions about the week without rules; and <u>interpreting</u>, <u>planning</u>, <u>deducting</u>, and <u>communicating</u> as he shares his discoveries at the Sharing Session. Based on this analysis of only <u>one</u> simple problem-solving activity, it becomes obvious that such activities do indeed provide opportunities for problem-solving skills practice!

In order to assure that <u>all</u> the problem-solving skills are being practiced and that the practice occurs as frequently as pssible, it is adviseable to "keep track" of the skills called for in each activity. When activities are written on cards or folders, the skills used can be listed on the card/folder. With tape-recorded activities, the skills list can be attached to the tape or placed on the tape case.

10. <u>When problem-solving activities are to be done independently, a materials list</u> should accompany each activity. This list may be written on the back of the problem-solving activity card/folder, or taped to the cassette tape case. Such lists are extremely helpful when the teacher or a student aide is "setting up" the activities in the classroom. In addition, students working independently can be given the responsibility for checking this list to determine if all the necessary materials are available.

SUMMARY:  In this unit we have explored the problem-solving method of instruction; what it is, how it s organized, when and how to present it in the classroom, and what to be aware of when developing problem-solving activities.  Emphasis was placed on the fact that simple problem-solving activities can serve as stepping stones to move the child from highly teacher-directed, teacher-oriented learning to more independent student-directed, student-oriented learning.  In Unit Six, problem-solving through inquiry is explored, which is yet another stepping stone in the move toward independent learning.

PART II: UNIT 6

THE METHOD OF PROBLEM-SOLVING THROUGH INQUIRY TEACHING
Sheila A. Wineman

## What is Inquiry?

Inquiry is a term which has become increasingly popular in all areas and at all levels of education. This focus on inquiry by such a wide range of people with such varied outlooks has made a succinct definition of the term almost impossible. In the area of social studies, however, most educators view inquiry as a method of problem solving which is based on rational thinking. When the social studies student is involved in inquiry, he is faced with a perplexing problem which he actively explores. He uses his own knowledge as well as outside resources and experiences to inquire into the problem and discover acceptable, rational solutions on his own. Active involvement is an essential element in this inquiry process. No longer does the student sit passively and receive information; i.e., listen to the teacher describe a problem and write down an explanation that contains solutions. Instead, the student becomes an active learner, a developer of information in his own right. He makes his own inquiries into the problem, discovers his own evidence, develops and tests his own hypotheses, and draws his own conclusions. The inquiry has been his, and the knowledge he has gained is meaningful, indeed!

## What Part do Problem Solving Skills, Concepts
## and Values Play in Inquiry Teaching?

Inquiry teaching strategies reflect a particular way of dealing with problem-solving skills, content and values. When inquiry strategies are used, emphasis is placed on helping students develop basic problem-solving skills which will allow them to make inquiries into problem situations and discover solutions for themselves. New or renewed values may result as the end product of the student's personal inquiry process, but the only value which is deliberately "taught" is the valuing of inquiry itself.

The development of problem solving skills is viewed as a major goal by inquiry-oriented teachers since these are the skills or procedures we use to deal with information when we think through problems and make decisions. Some of the most commonly identified problem solving skills are:

| | |
|---|---|
| analyzing | generalizing |
| classifying | hypothesizing |
| contrasting | interpreting |
| comparing | inferring |
| defining | integrating |
| describing | observing |
| evaluating | predicting |
| experimenting | synthesizing |

As students learn to use these problem solving skills more effectively, they become better able to confront problem situations, process information related to the problem, systematically test their insights and ideas as to possible solutions, and finally, determine a satisfactory solution which has personal meaning.

The content of the social studies program as viewed by an inquiry-oriented teacher is very different from the body of knowledge considered to be "necessary learning" by some social studies educators. In inquiry teaching, content becomes the vehicle for the problem solving process. The students and/or the teacher identify a relevant problem for consideration and, as a result of inquiries into the problem, students interact with data from the social sciences, humanities, social issues and value questions and discover basic concepts and generalizations. In some cases, the teacher may present pre-determined problem situations which are geared to the discovery of specific concepts. Regardless of "who" identifies "what" problem, content remains an important element since one must have something to "problem-solve" about!

As stated above, the values dimension of the inquiry approach is not geared toward the promotion of a given set of values which is considered acceptable in our society. Instead, students are encouraged to inquire into problem situations which are often (if not usually) the result of values conflicts, consider alternative ways of thinking about and dealing with these problems, and consider the possible consequences of their decisions. Through this procedure, students come to value the inquiry process itself and often develop new values as a result of the insights and information gained.

## Why is Inquiry Important?

In addition to the meaningful knowledge gained from the inquiry experience, there are other benefits which should be noted. The sense of achievement and personal satisfaction which comes when students solve problems on their own can increase self-confidence and make them much less hesitant to tackle future problems. In many instances, students will be motivated to the degree that they will actively seek out new problems to solve, as well as become more aware of existing problems which they have felt inadequte to deal with in the past. This increased awareness of problems and willingness to deal with them, along with the improvement of problem solving skills brought about by practice and meaningful repetition, are benefits which cannot be overlooked.

Also worth noting is the fact that students who are exposed to a wide range of inquiry experiences often develop questioning attitudes toward information they receive and experiences they have. Rather than automatically accepting the word of an "authority" as "Truth," they will seek other sources to verify what has been said. Likewise, they may weigh an experience, re-think the "knowns" and "unknowns," and evaluate several alternatives before they decide on a course of action. Such reflection thinking can only help them further along the road to becoming rational, independent decision-makers and problem solvers not only in social studies, but hopefully in all phases of their lives.

## How is the Inquiry Process Conducted in the Classroom?

Now that you are aware of the "what" and "why" of inquiry, you are ready to proceed to the "how." How is the inquiry process conducted in the classroom? Are there certain steps one should follow, and if so, what is involved in each of these steps?

As defined in this unit, the five steps in the inquiry process are:

1. Experience a problem situation.

2. Define the problem.

3. Develop hypotheses.

4. Test the hypotheses.

5. Develop a conclusion.

The following section provides an explanation and example of each of these steps.

I.  Experience a problem situation.

A.  Example:  You and your students have been studying the early
growth and development of our country.  As the result of class
discussions, films, "You Were There" presentations by small
groups, and readings from the text and other reference books,
the students have a good deal of information about the condition
of our country in the 1700's.  In an attempt to help the students
gain further insight into the "hows" and "whys" of events during
that time, you decide to present an inquiry problem for them
to explore.  You enter the classroom dressed in the style of
the 1700's.  You tell the students that you are John Peter Zenger
and that you are in jail because you printed articles criticizing the colonial government in the New York Weekly Journal.
You explain the circumstances and events leading to your arrest
and make your exit, asking the students to review you case and
decide if your arrest and trial were legally justified.

B.  Explanation:  In order for inquiry to occur, the students must
be confronted with a problem situation or issue which raises
questions and causes a degree of confusion or uncertainty--a
situation which casts doubt on something they thought they
knew, understood, believed or valued.  In other words, they
must become personally involved with the problem situation in
order for inquiry to take place.  Conversely, if the teacher
presents a situation which she sees as a problem, but which
the students don't identify with or become involved in, then
the resulting study is simply the study of a problem (the
teacher's problem, to be exact) and not an inquiry experience.

In the example above, the teacher has provided an interesting,
motivating role playing experience which has involved the
students in a problem situation.  Sharing a news article,
viewing a film, listening to a tape, taking a short walking
field trip, or discussing an argument that occurred at lunch
could be equally effective inquiry-starters, as long as the
students become personally involved.  Obviously, student-
initiated problem situations can also be excellent inquiry-
starters.

II.  Define the problem

    A.    Example:  You (the teacher) return to the classroom and a
barrage of questions!  Was Zenger a real person?  Was he
really put in jail just because he didn't like what was
happening in the government and said so?  What did he
really say in his articles?  Was he hanged?

After a brief discussion of the role playing, the questions
raised and the information provided, you summarize the
problem by stating, "Based on the role play you just observed,
the problem to be solved is whether or not the arrest
and trial of John Peter Zenger were legally justified."
You then use the following questions to guide the students
as they define and clarify the problem for themselves:

    1.    What are all the things you can tell me about the problem?
Zenger was a real person who lived in the 1700's.
He wrote articles criticizing the government.  He
was sent to jail and had a jury trial.  (Sample student
responses)

    2.    What are some things you think may be true about the
problem?
Putting Zenger in jail was unfair.  He had a right
to express his views.

    3.    What are some things you're not sure about (or don't
know) in relation to the problem?
Do we have an accurate account of what happened
to Zenger?  Do we have "both sides of the story?
Was the information he printed in his articles
true?

    4.    What is the exact problem we're going to solve?
(Students define the problem in their own words)
Was the arrest and trial of John Peter Zenger
legally justified?

    B.    Explanation:  The procedure of defining the problem and bring-
ing it into focus takes the students one step further
in making the problem their own and involving them in
the inquiry process, since they are conducting a personal
examination of their knowledge and understanding in relation
to the problem.  During this defining phase, the discussion

should be directed toward a review of what they learned during the problem presentation and possible personal knowledge they may have about the problem situation. Identifying possible solutions comes in the next step.

III. Develop Hypotheses

A. Example: You and your students review all the information and thoughts you have about John Peter Zenger and the students offer a hypothesis or hypotheses. (What are all the things we know about Zenger? What pieces of information are most important in relation to our stated problem? What other things do we know about the law and free speech that we can consider? With all this in mind, do you feel that the arrest, jailing and trial were justified? Does everyone agree? If not, what are your other hypotheses?)

Two hypotheses are offered by the students:

1. Zenger's arrest, jailing and trail cannot be legally justified.

2. Zenger's arrest, jailing and trial can be legally justified.

B. Explanation: Hypothesizing involves the students in determining a tentative answer to the problem they defined in Step Two--that is, they are making an educated guess based on the information they have and past experience. In fact, when they formulate their hypothesis, they are not only considering the evidence and information they have at hand, but the evidence and information they expect to find as well. Thus, the hypothesis includes the bits of information available along with as yet unexamined evidence.

It is crucial that students understand that a hypothesis is tentative and that further examination of evidence may result in its rejection. In fact, they may formulate and reject several hypotheses before they identify one which they can validate. This procedure of formulating, testing and either validating or rejecting hypotheses is a basic part of the inquiry process.

IV. Test the Hypotheses

A. Example: After being placed in groups according to which hypothesis they support, the students examine and evaluate all the information available about Zenger and his trial. Among the pieces of evidence you (the teacher) help them gather are: records describing the procedure of the trial, history texts giving accounts of Zenger's experience, copies of Zenger's articles published in the New York Weekly Journal, rebuttals written by the governor which appeared as billboards at the time, copies of personal letters written by Zenger to his wife during his jail term, the memoirs of Attorney General Richard Bradley, the prosecutor in Zenger's trial, a copy of the speech made to the trial jury by Andrew Hamilton, Zenger's lawyer, and a copy of the Bill of Rights.

As the students examine and evaluate the evidence, they ask themselves questions, such as: Is this relevant? Is it authentic? Is it accurate? Does it coincide with other pieces of evidence? Is this fact or opinion? Does this piece of evidence merely reflect the biases and prejudices of the author? How does the evidence fit togehter? Does it support our hypothesis?

B. Explanation: Testing the hypothesis involves students in examining and evaluating the available evidence. In the example above, the students were given assistance in the evidence-gathering procedure, but in another inquiry situation, this procedure might be their responsibility alone. Also, in the example, the evidence was primarily in written form, whereas in other instances, the students might rely more heavily on observation, listening, discussion with an expert, or recall in gathering their evidence. The problem might be one which would allow the students to test the hypotheses by actually performing some task or activity (e.g., actually trying their ideas as to possible solutions to keeping the playground litter-free). Obviously, the problem being explored will dictate the type of testing which will be appropriate.

74

Questioning plays a vital part in this step of the inquiry process. Regardless of whether the questions originate with the students (as in the example above) or the teacher, or whether they are oral or in the form of written study guides, they are vital in moving the students toward a decision in this testing procedure.

V. Develop and Share a Conclusion

A. Example: After reviewing all the evidence available and organizing their information, each "hypothesis group" presents its findings in the form of a television "news flash." With this particular problem, the "reporter" for each hypothesis group delivers basically the same report (findings):

1. Based on factual evidence about Governor Cosby's past and his term as governor, the articles printed by Zenger presented true information.

2. The charge of seditious libel was unjustified.

3. Even though the Bill of Rights had not yet been adopted, Zenger should have been allowed to present the truth to the people.

A total group discussion follows the reports and the students then vote to determine (conclude) which hypothesis was valid. They conclude that the arrest, jailing and trial of John Peter Zenger was not legally justified.

In order to apply and share the conclusion voted best, each small group identifes another situation during the 1700's which they feel may (or may not!) reflect a "miscarriage of justice." The small groups investigate their chosen situation and choose a creative way to present their findings to the total group during a Sharing Session.

B. Explanation: A conclusion is the target of the inquiry process. Keeping in mind the results obtained in testing the hypothesis, the students summarize their findings and attempt to state them in a clear, concise manner. This statement reflects the validity or invalidity of the original hypothesis. In the example above, one group of students found their hypothesis to be valid, and after hearing the "report" from this group and discussing the findings, the second group agreed to the validity of the hypothesis. When such agreement occurs, the students may proceed one step further and apply the conclusion to new data. If, on the other hand, the conclusion indicates that the hypotheses are invalid, they can either be modified or discarded and new hypotheses developed. In either case, a worthwhile learning experience will undoubtedly have occurred through the inquiry process.

Many teachers are aware of the method of problem-solving through inquiry and they make sincere attempts to involve their students in the step-by-step process described in the preceeding section. However, simply "putting students through the steps" does not guarantee that they are truly involved in inquiry. Let's consider Mr. X as an example. Mr. X identifies issues or problem situations which he feels are vitally important. He provides specific supporting evidence, he directs his students as they analyze the evidence, and he leads them to his conclusions. Mr. X has followed the inquiry procedure, but he has not involved his students in inquiry! True, his students have been involved in a problem-solving exercise which may be valuable and they have made some useful discoveries (predetermined by Mr. X), but they have not had an inquiry experience.

The essence of inquiry lies in student ownership of the problem to be explored; that is, the problem must become the students' problem. In order for this ownership to occur, the students must view the problem as one which conflicts with their needs, interests, or beliefs; in other words, their values. When they actually feel this conflict, then the problem and the need to resolve it become theirs, and inquiry can occur. The following example may further clarify this point. In Ms. Z's social studies class, she regularly discusses social issues with her students and she is well aware of those topics which represent "real problems" to them. Based on this knowledge, she presents a problem situation in class which she knows will elicit a "gut-level" reaction (i.e., they will be confused and concerned because doubt has been cast on something they thought they knew, understood, believed, or valued). Ms. Z assists the students in defining the problem as they see it; she provides some guidance as they develop and test their hypotheses; and she gives them the freedom to develop their own conclusions. In this example, Ms. Z has demonstrated an understanding of the essence of inquiry. Although she provides

some degree of structure by identifying the nature of the problem to be invest-
igated, the students have the responsibility of choosing the specific problem
which they will resolve and the proceed with their own inquiries and conclusions.

## When Is Inquiry Teaching Used in the Classroom?

Inquiry teaching can be used with virtually any social studies topic.
However, some basic considerations should be kept in mind in determining when
to use inquiry.  For example, many students are accustomed to structured
situations where they take a relatively passive role in the learning process.
In some cases, the major focus of their social studies learning experiences
may have been teacher-directed lecture/discussion sessions, or reading and
discussion of the text, followed by answering the questions at the end of
each chapter.  Thus, they may be totally unprepared for the freedom and
responsibility inherent in inquiry.  If they are expected to walk into the
classroom on Day One, plunge enthusiastically into a problem (even a problem
which is "real" to them), and breeze through the inquiry process, there's a
strong likelihood that they will feel inadequte and unprepared to meet the
challenge and this initial "failure" may severely inhibit their receptiveness
and enthusiasm for future inquiry experiences.  Teachers who hold such expectations
for their students may also experience feelings of failure and a hesitancy
to provide further opportunities for inquiry.

Involving students in simple problem-solving activities which provide a
degree of structure and teacher direction and then moving gradually into less
controlled inquiry experiences is often advisable simply because that's "where
the students are" when they come to us.  Simple problem-solving activities can
be used to assist the students in moving from teacher-directed to self-directed
learning, which is a goal of inquiry teaching.

With increased confidence in their ability to solve problems and a clearer
understanding of the problem-solving approach to learning, students can generally
make a smooth transition from simple problem-solving to inquiry activities.  Once
this transition is made, they will be eager to tackle new and different topics
through inquiry experiences.  Inquiry lesson plans can be put to excellent use
at this point.  Based on an understanding of student interests and needs, the
teacher can identify inquiry experiences which will involve students with the topic.
Needless to say, the teacher cannot preplan the students' definitions of the
problem, their hypotheses, or their conclusions, but some "educated guesses"
can be made as to what their responses will be and planning can proceed and
materials be gathered accordingly.

One final consideration which should be kept in mind is related to the old idea that it's possible "to get too much of a good thing." When students get "hooked" on inquiry, they tend to want to do inquiry activities and nothing else! If they become bored with inquiry, then they may not "tune in" and "own" the problem, and as we've noted previously, inquiry will not occur. To avoid this problem, it's advisable to involve students in a variety of other experiences along with the inquiry activities. Consider, for example, the topic of the problems and needs of senior citizens. What varied experiences could be provided along with inquiry activities? One example might be having the students view a film which identifies some of the special needs of this age group and writing their own narative for the film. The film and student narrative could be shared at a P.T.A. "Parent Awareness" meeting. Another example might be visiting a rest home, talking with the residents, getting first-hand information on their problems and needs, and developing a community newsletter to send home to parents listing "special things we can do for special people." A third example might be a "Senior Friends Day," when elderly friends are invited to visit school and "walk through" part of the day with the students. Experiences such as these could prevent boredom with inquiry activities as well as provide valuable alternative learning experiences.

## Summary

In this unit, you have explored the "what," "why," "how," and "when" of inquiry teaching--what it is, why it's important, how it's conducted in the classroom, and when it should be used. Although you now have a general idea of what inquiry is all about, the chapters which follow will provide a closer look at some tpics which are directly related to the inquiry process. The problem solving skills which can be developed and refined through inquiry are examined in Part II, Unit 5 and questioning, which is an essential element in inquiry is explored in detail in Unit 7. A sample plan for a lesson which focuses on inquiry is provided in Part III, Unit 2.

78

## PART II: UNIT 7
## IDENTIFYING AND WRITING BEHAVIORAL OBJECTIVES
James L. Barth

You may be wondering why there is a chapter on objectives in a unit on evaluation. Surely you expected examples of test questions. But think for a moment which comes first when planning a lesson, your objectives or your test questions? The purpose of the unit is to illustrate the role of objectives as they relate to evaluation.

What are the purposes of having objectives for any activity?
(Write a short response here)


What would be some of your objectives for teaching social studies? For example helping your students to be good citizens. What would two other behavioral objectives be?

1.


2.


What are objectives? Why are they necessary?

Imagine that the Jones family wanted to go on a vacation but they could not decide where to go. If they packed the car and left on their vacation without having picked a destination, what direction would they go? What road would they take? Of course, this is a ridiculous situation. Almost as ridiculous would be for the Jones family to decide that they were going "East" for a vacation. "East" could be anywhere from the Florida Keys to Maine. Although a general direction would be some help in planning a trip, it certainly would not help them in making advanced hotel reservations or in deciding the proper clothes and sports equipment to pack. On the other hand, if the Jones family decided to go to New York City to see the Mets play baseball and to go to some Broadway plays, then they would be able to select a specific route, make reservations, and take the proper clothes and equipment.

How does this example compare with the objectives of a teacher?


*This chapter was originally published in Methods of Instruction in Social Studies Education, by James Barth (Washington, D.D.: University Press of America, 1979). It has been revised for purposes of this text.

Why does a teacher need objectives?

What are some advantages of specific objectives as opposed to general objectives?

Many teachers consider the development of "good citizenship" as a general objective. List what you believe teachers mean by this term—that is what are some of the characteristics of "good citizenship."

1.

2.

3.

Do the characteristics you have listed above actually help you select content or determine your behavior as a teacher?
Circle either      YES    or    NO
Explain:

Here is a frequently spoken objective of many social studies teachers: "I'd like my students to <u>understand</u> the Industrial Revolution in this country." Does the word <u>understand</u> as used above have a precise meaning? If I said to you, "You should understand the Industrial Revolution," would you know precisely what was expected of you?
Circle either      YES    or    No
Explain:

     Let us look at objectives more closely. Most teachers have some objectives for teaching their courses. They are really not quite as confused as the Jones family. However, teachers' objectives are often very general and sometimes their goals are in conflict. If the teacher teaches social studies and her objective is to "develop good citizenship," this is somewhat like the Jones family saying that they are going "East." It provides the teacher with no specific guides as to what content to select, what methods or techniques to use, what assignments to make to the students, or how to evaluate the students in relation to the objectives. As the Jones family might spend their vacation wandering all around the "East" without much satisfaction, the teacher might spend her year wandering all around "good citizenship" with equal lack of satisfaction.

Some teachers list several objectives for their teaching, but often they are in conflict. For example, a teacher might say, "I want my students to learn to accept authority and to do things the right way," and also say "I want my students to become independent, critical thinkers." How should this teacher behave in the classroom: should she demand that her view be accepted—this is accepting authority—and that things be done the "right" way? If so, does this develop independent thinking?

Teachers frequently verbalize a goal such as "developing independent or critical thinkers." But, if one looks at their behavior, the goal they have really accepted and use in the classroom is the passive acceptance of authority. This is an illustration of a teacher verbalizing goals at one level and actually operating in the classroom on another set of goals. This, we would maintain, is an improper use of objectives. Now we should like to emphasize a more philosophically desirable way of thinking about goals.

Let us review general characteristics of good objectives:
1. They should give both the teacher and the student a sense of direction.
2. They should guide the teacher in selecting materials, techniques, and strategies of teaching.
3. They should prove guides for teaching behavior.
4. They should not be in conflict with one another.

There is a fifth characteristic. In order to determine whether the students have reached the objective or not, the objective should be stated in such a way that the teacher can measure student behavior in relation to the objective. Objectives of this type are called behavioral objectives. What is the sense of having a specific objective that can not be evaluated? How can the teacher determine whether the student has become a "good citizen" or an "independent thinker?"

## Write Your Own Behavioral Objective

Perhaps you already know how to write complete behavioral objectives. You should have a chance to demonstrate your knowledge and skill. Please circle the appropriate response:

    a.   I don't know anything about writing a complete behavioral objective, but I will try to write one in the box below.

    b.   I know something about writing objectives but I am not sure I can write a complete objective.  I will try to write an objective below anyway.

    c.   Yes, I know how to write a complete behavioral objective and just to prove the point I will write one in the following box.

<br>

## Checking Objective Against Three Criteria

Any complete behavioral objective fulfills three criteria.  Check the objective you write in the box against these three criteria.  Check the criteria if you have fulfilled it in your objective.

    \_\_\_\_\_ Criteria One:   Is there an observable behavior?

    \_\_\_\_\_ Criteria Two:   Are the conditions for the behavior specified?

    \_\_\_\_\_ Criteria Three:   Are criteria for acceptable performance included?

EXAMPLE:   for example your objective should look and sound something like this:

Having viewed the film strip "Westward Ho" and read
           (conditions    for    behavior)

Chapter Four of the text, students will be able to

identify in a small discussion group four to six reasons
(observable behavior)              (acceptable performance)

for the westward movement.

If you have not included all three of these criteria; observable behavior, conditions, and acceptable performance, then your objective is not complete.  If you have not written a complete objective what you should do now is review the following explanation of each of the three criteria.

Criteria One:

Does your objective include a behavior you want to observe when the student has completed the lesson?

"The student will be able to identify through discussion. . . ."

"The student will be able to write. . . ."

Observable behaviors other than <u>identifying</u> and <u>writing</u> are: listing, reciting, contrasting, discriminating, and to compare and contrast.

Now try your skill at writing out an observable behavior using one of the suggestions above.

```
┌──────────────────────────────────────────────────────────────────┐
│                                                                    │
│                                                                    │
│                                                                    │
│                                                                    │
│                                                                    │
└──────────────────────────────────────────────────────────────────┘
```

Criteria Two:

Does your behavioral objective include the conditions under which the student is expected to perform the desired behavior?

"<u>After</u> <u>listening</u> <u>in</u> <u>class</u> <u>to</u> <u>the</u> <u>audio</u> <u>tape</u> with statements by the Supreme Court Justices, the students will be able to identify through discussion. . . ."

"<u>After</u> <u>completing</u> <u>one</u> <u>of</u> <u>the</u> <u>selected</u> <u>readings</u> on class list the student will be able to write. . . ."

Now try your skill at writing out the conditions under which the student is expected to perform.

```
┌──────────────────────────────────────────────────────────────────┐
│                                                                    │
│                                                                    │
│                                                                    │
│                                                                    │
└──────────────────────────────────────────────────────────────────┘
```

Criteria Three:

Finally, does your objective specify the criteria for acceptable performance?

"After listening to the class tape with statements by the Supreme Court Justices, the student will be able to identify through discussions, <u>three</u> <u>of</u> <u>the</u> <u>four</u> <u>judges'</u> <u>opinions</u> <u>concerning</u> <u>wiretapping</u>."

"After completing one of the selected readings on class list, the student will be able to write a one page paper describing at least two court cases <u>with</u> <u>100%</u> <u>accuracy</u>."

Now try your skill at writing out criteria for acceptable behavior.

```



```

## Checking Yourself Out

Can you identify complete behavioral objectives? Let's find out. Read the following six objectives. Mark each one either complete or incomplete. If the objective is incomplete explain why. (For correct answers see page 78 )

1. _____ After participating in the "trust walk" each student will write his definition of trust in one sentence. (explain if incomplete)

2. _____ Having viewed the film "Black Prophets," you will be able to discuss in a small group three of the four Black leaders and their views. (explain if incomplete)

3. _____ The student will be able to define 80% of the anthropological terms. (explain if incomplete)

4. _____ Given the latest issue of Know Your World, the students will write and present a newscast. (explain if incomplete)

5. _____ Given the in class reading "Voices in the Soviet" the student will understand three of the five Russian authors known for their dissent. (explain if incomplete)

6. _____ Given the taped speeches of presidential candidates, the student will list three differences in the two major platforms with 80% accuracy. (explain if necessary)

## Write One Complete Behavioral Objective

The proof is in the doing. So, having completed the above series of exercises you should be ready to demonstrate that you can write a complete behavioral objective. Keeping in mind the three criteria, write one complete behavioral objective on any social studies topic.

Three Levels of Questions:
Knowledge, Skills, Attitudes

If you have mastered the skill of writing complete behavioral objectives, then you ought to feel a sense of accomplishment for now you are almost ready to write lesson and unit plans and construct test questions. Almost ready because you still must master the skill of identifying and writing the three different levels of objectives. The three levels of objectives are: knowledge, skill, and attitude. In this final section of this unit you are expected to identify and write objectives that are classified as one of the three levels.

For example:

(Knowledge Objective) Having read Chapter Three in the history text, students will identify and list three of the five generals named.

(Skill Objective) Having selected an individual topic, students will demonstrate research skills by completing the required topic outline.

(Attitude Ovjective) Students having studied the American Revolution will demonstrate a critical (open-minded) attitude toward revolutions in a short written exercise.

Did you notice how the three levels of objectives differed from each other. All three levels met the criteria of complete hehavioral objectives, but they differ on the type of behavior called for. One calls for the listing of information (cognitive memory), one calls for the demonstration of a skill, and the third requires the demonstration of a particular attitude (affective). At this point you need both more examples of the different levels and practice writing at these different levels.

Knowledge Behavioral Objective
Knowledge objectives normally call for the recall of specific

information, so this objective often includes such words as: recite, list, write, identify, and differentiate. This level of objective often calls for the lower levels of thinking such as cognitive-memory and convergent responses. Examples are:

"After reading the article from Time, December 20, 1972, the student will be able to write in class two reasons for continued U.S. involvement in Viet Nam."

"After seeing the film 'Nicholas and Alexandra' the student will identify a personality characteristic of Nicholas and compare it with the characteristic of one other European monarch (your choice) in a two page paper."

Now try your skill at writing out a knowledge behavioral objective.

## Skill Behavior Objective

Normally daily lessons and units require students to practice specific skills. For example if you ask the student to read a paragraph and identify the main idea, you are literally asking the student to practice the skill of reading. Other skills which have been traditionally practiced are writing, (note-taking, essay, research), speaking, studying, and grouping. Examples are:

"Having reviewed the SQ3R technique, student will improve their reading skills by reading orally in class following the SQ3R technique."

"Using the library, the student will demonstrate research skills by selecting five sources and writing a 200 word theme on the dilemma of pollution in Cuyahoga County"

Now try your skill at writing out a skill behavioral objective.

86

## Attitude Behavioral Objective

Your lesson and unit planning not only call for knowledge and skill but often implicitly call for students to acquire a particular attitude.  For example history teachers often say "I want my students to like history."  In precise behavioral terms the history teacher in reality means "I want my students to have a positive attitude toward history."  In fact, one can measure whether students have a positive or negative attitude toward history or for that matter toward any subject.  Attitudes other than positive or negative which teachers wish students to acquire are:  open-mindedness, (critical thinking), willingness, self-confidence, respect for others or tolerance, and cooperativeness.

Examples are:

"Having been placed into small groups for the study of Chapter III, students will demonstrate in their small groups a cooperative attitude."

"While a student is showing an individual project, students will demonstrate an attitude of respect for others by listening to the presentation."

"After studying conflicting historical evidence found in the Jack Dawes Kit the student will demonstrate in class discussion a critical attitude toward historical events."

Now try your skill at writing out an attitude behavioral objective.

## Have you made a discovery?

You may have discovered by now that one behavioral objective may contain several levels of behavior.  It is not uncommon to find knowledge and skill level behaviors in the same objective.  "Students will recall in class discussion important points from a lecture by following the proper note-taking form."  This behavioral objective includes both knowledge which is the recall and skill which is note-taking.  "While working on small group skills students will demonstrate the attitude of respect for others by adopting a cooperative attitude."  In this case both group skills and the attitudes of respect and cooperation are combined into one objective. So what should you conclude? You should conclude that the three levels of objectives can be stated separately or they can be combined into one objective.

The Final Check on Your Skill at Identifying Complete Behavioral Objectives

Listed below are eight objectives on the topic "developing good citizenship." Mark each one either complete or incomplete and circle and appropriate level or levels, K - knowledge, S - skills, A - attitude. See page 79 for correct answers.

1. _____ Having studied the Constitution, students will know the respon-
   K  S  A  sibilities of a good citizen. (explain if incomplete)

2. _____ Having studied the Bill of Rights, students will demonstrate in
   K  S  A  their personal relations with others the attitude of respect.

3. _____ Students, in their study of democracy, will demonstrate their
   K  S  A  research skills by listing a brief bibliography on the subject.
            (explain if incomplete)

4. _____ Students will learn to appreciate the advantages of being a
   K  S  A  citizen in this country. (explain if incomplete)

5. _____ The values of a democracy will become known as students think
   K  S  A  about what they enjoy as guarantees. (explain if incomplete)

6. _____ Students in small groups while studying the Bill or Rights, will
   K  S  A  show by their rating on an evaluation form their positive
            attitude toward group cooperation. (explain if incomplete)

7. _____ In chapter seven of the text, students will identify and ex-
   K  S  A  plain two of the three major concepts as part of a unit test.
            (explain if incomplete)

8. _____ Students, having studied the Constitution, should really under-
   K  S  A  stand and fully appreciate and finally have faith in the wisdom
            of the founding fathers. (explain if incomplete)

ANSWERS

Check Yourself Out (page 74 )

1. Complete
2. Complete
3. Incomplete because objective is missing Criteria Two (conditions under
     which the student is expected to perform).
4. Complete
5. Incomplete because Criteria One (observable behavior) is improperly
     stated. "Understand" cannot be measured or observed.

6. Complete

Final Check    (page 78 )

1. Incomplete (K) because Criteria One (observable behavior) is improperly
   stated.
2. Complete (A)
3. Complete (S)
4. Incomplete (A) because Criteria One (observable behavior) is improperly
   stated.  "To appreciate" cannot be measured or observed.  Criteria
   Two (conditions) and Criteria Three (acceptable performance) are
   missing.
5. Incomplete (A) because Criteria One (observable behavior) is improperly
   stated.  "Become known" cannot be measured or observed.  Criteria
   Two (conditions) and Criteria Three (acceptable performance) are
   missing.
6. Complete (A)
7. Complete (K)
8. Incomplete (K,A) because Criteria One (observable behavior) is improperly
   stated.  "Really understand, fully appreciate," and "have faith"
   cannot be measured or observed.  Criteria Three (acceptable performance) is missing.

PART II: UNIT 8

DEVELOPMENT OF QUESTIONING SKILLS

James L. Barth

Purpose: Having completed this unit on questioning, you should be able to identify the four different types of questions by demonstrating the ability to correctly construct examples of each.

## Introduction

We wouldn't argue that there are many skills necessary for effective social studies teaching. However, one of the most important skills that a social studies teacher ought to have is the ability to ask effective questions. It does seem that social studies teachers spend much of their class time, at least thirty percent, in either lecture or recitation. Recitation includes both question and answer and discussion. Now, draw a distinction between these two forms of recitation. In a question and answer type session, the teacher directs questions toward students who normally answer the teacher so that it is a one to one exchange. In a discussion, the teachers attempt to engage students in a dialogue not only between themselves and students but also between students. We are all familiar with the pattern where the question and answer technique is used primarily to check students' specific knowledge. A discussion is usually used to stimulate students' personal judgment about events such as one would find in a Socratic discussion, where students and teacher challenge each other. If it is true that much social studies class time is devoted to asking questions, then it is extremely important that you learn about the basic kinds of questions that can be asked. Three sections make up this chapter. The first section is identifying and writing the four different questions, the second section is applying the four types of questions, and the final section measures your attitude toward the four types of questions.

Identifying and Writing the Four
Different Questions

Instructions: There are three parts to this section. Each type of question has an introduction, some examples, and an identification practice. At the end of the lesson is a self-test which you should take to check your understanding of the four types of questions. Now proceed with the chapter.

*This chapter was originally published in Methods of Instruction in Social Studies Education, by James L. Barth (Washington, D.C., University Press of America, 1979). It has been revised for the purposes of this text.

Cognitive-Memory Questions

Cognitive-memory questions tend to be restricted to the lowest levels of thinking. Questions of this type seek answers which usually require students to reproduce factual information or definitions relying on recall or recognition skills only. Responses tend to be short phrases or merely a single word. Pupils respond to cognitive-memory questions by recalling a fact, defining a term, noting something they observe, or simply giving an answer based on rote memory. Usually the cognitive-memory question calls for one and only one right answer, i.e., What year did Columbus discover America? Answer: 1492. The following questions are typical of the types of cognition elicited by cognitive-memory questions.

Example Questions

A. Identify what the letters NRA stand for?
B. What is the largest state in the Union?
C. Was Franklin D. Roosevelt elected President four times?
D. According to the film, what are the major contributors to atmospheric pollution?
E. How would you classify King Henry VIII: as a constitutional or absolute monarch?
F. Recall who was President during the Civil War?
G. Name the first President of the United States?

To improve your skill in identifying cognitive-memory(CM) questions, read each of the questions below. In the blank provided, write CM if you think the question belongs in this category. If you decide that a question does not belong to this category then label it N. After classifying each question read the paragraph that follows to check your answer.

Identification Practice (please mark your answer in the space provided)

_____ A. Who was the first person to walk on the moon?
_____ B. Tell me why you think China is important?
_____ C. How would you explain Henry Kissinger's success as a diplomat?
_____ D. Recall when the Constitution of the United States was ratified?
_____ E. Identify the country that has the highest suicide rate?
_____ F. Did the Russian Revolution start in 1917?

If you marked questions A, D, E, F as cognitive-memory questions, then you are on the right track. These four questions ask students merely to reproduce factual information such as names or dates. Although clear distinctions are sometimes difficult to make, questions B and C probably are intended to have the student <u>develop</u> <u>a</u> <u>definition</u> or engage in <u>specula-tion</u>.

Key words when writing cognitive-memory questions

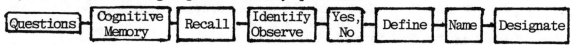

### Writing Practice

It is time for you to try your hand at writing this type question. In the space provided below write three cognitive-memory questions. Choose any topic you wish. Use the chart above as a reference for the different cognitive activities generally stimulated by cognitive-memory questions.

1.

2.

3.

## Convergent Questions

In this category, questions require students to establish a relation-ship between facts or ideas in order to construct a response. Convergent questions, as the label for this category suggests, are aimed at eliciting one "right" or "best" answer. Generally the information necessary for answering such questions is assumed to be known by both the teacher and the student. The task for the student involves recalling certain facts or ideas, organizing or associating them in some manner, and formulating an explanation <u>in</u> <u>his</u> <u>own</u> <u>words</u>. To cope with this type of question the stu-dent is required to perform cognitive operations that are more complex than those needed in the previous category. Explaining, comparing, contrasting, relating, and association are the specific types of cognitive behavior connected with convergent questions. Usually convergent questions call for an answer that is right or best but put in the student's own words, i.e., Why did Columbus want to sail to India? There is a right answer to this question. A student can give the answer in his own words.

### Example Questions

    A. Contrast the weapons of World War I with those of World War II?
    B. Why did the South lose the Civil War?
    C. How are the countries of Great Britain and Japan similar?

D. Explain why under developed countries like Peru are unable to modernize?

E. Why has the Communist Party been successful in Italy and not in Greece?

F. How can the Congress of the United States influence the domestic policies of the President?

G. Compare TV with radio?

From the examples it is obvious that "how," "why," "compare and contrast" tend to act as cues for identifying this type of question. Research studies have demonstrated that student thinking can become inhibited if convergent questions are utilized constantly. Students assume the purpose of instruction is strictly one of finding the right answers and may become very defensive when challenged to think for themselves.

In the set of questions below, use the letters CM, C or N to indicate whether the question is cognitive-memory, convergent, or neither. The following paragraph will give you the correct answers.

Identification Practice (please mark your answers in the space provided)

_____ A. Why did the Americans occupy the Phillipine Islands after the Spanish-American War?

_____ B. What is the official name of the KKK?

_____ C. What priority should the government put on eliminating poverty?

_____ D. Name the three branches of the national government?

_____ E. How is the present economic condition of a peasant in Malaysia different from his ancestors who lived 1000 years ago?

_____ F. What was the relationship between the English and German monarchies during World War I?

_____ G. How are China and Russia alike?

Your task of identifying the different types of questions in this set was more difficult. If you marked questions A, E, F, and G as convergent, you are progressing nicely. The use of How and Why should have alerted you on three of these questions. Questions B and D are representative of the cognitive-memory category, while item C should have been marked N. If you identified these questions correctly move on to the next section. If you missed one or two, take a minute to review.

Key words when writing convergent questions

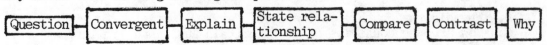

Writing Practice

Use the appropriate space below to write out three convergent type questions.

1.

2.

3.

Where have we been?

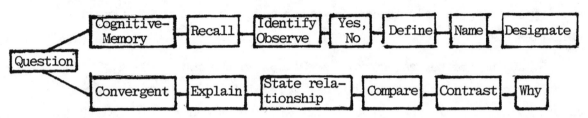

Divergent Questions

The questions in this next category provide the student with much more freedom and independence of response. As the title of this category suggests, divergent questions allow for a variety of answers. It is more difficult to predict the actual response a student might give. This type of question is often considered to be one that is thought-provoking. Teachers who pose divergent questions to their students are seeking original or creative responses. Divergent questions often confront students with problem situations which force them to combine facts and ideas in new ways in order to construct a viable solution. Predicting, hypothesizing, and inferring are the cognitive operations typical of this category. Usually divergent responses are based on well founded, valid, accurate information, but there are no right answers only plausible and sometimes best responses, i.e., What effect will the space program have on the future of the country?

Example Questions

A. What effect would the elimination of the private automobile as a means of transportation have on our lives?
B. How might the U.S. improve her relations with Cuba?
C. If you were free to choose where you wanted to live, where would it be?
D. How would our country be different if Congress consisted of only The House of Representatives?
E. What will urban life be like in twenty years if crime continues to increase at its present rate?

It is obvious that divergent questions demand more imagination and insight to answer than those of the preceding categories. This type of question tends to stimulate and to motivate the interests of students. Questions in this category encourage students to speculate and to explore topics in more depth, the result often being a greater appreciation and a more favorable attitude toward the subject matter. Too often teachers become so concerned about how much material they are covering that they neglect this type of question altogether. Consequently, they miss a valuable opportunity to help students develop and to extend their cognitive abilities.

By adding another category of questions to the model, the task of correctly classifying each one becomes more difficult. Read each question carefully and fill in the blanks in the space provided with either CM for cognitive-memory, C for convergent, D for divergent or N.

Identification Practice (please mark your answers in the space provided)

_____ A. What do you hypothesize the impact of Watergate will be on the Presidency?
_____ B. Was Hitler head of the German government during World War II?
_____ C. How might World War II have been shortened?
_____ D. Why have Mexican-American workers had trouble forming effective labor unions?
_____ E. What would you predict would happen to the U.S. if each state began establishing trade barriers?
_____ F. What effect will the oil shortage most probably have on the country?
_____ G. Compare the governments of Spain and Italy?

If you selected items A, C, E, and F as being divergent questions, you are correct. These questions would engage the student in hypothesizing and predicting. Question B, however, only requires recall and a yes or no answer. If you marked questions D and G as being convergent, you are doing well.

Key words when writing divergent questions

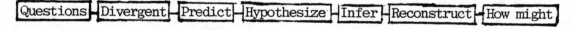

Questions – Divergent – Predict – Hypothesize – Infer – Reconstruct – How might

Writing practice

If you really want to test your skill, try rephrasing some of the questions you have already written so that they will fit this new category.

Write three divergent questions.

1.

2.

3.

Where have we been?

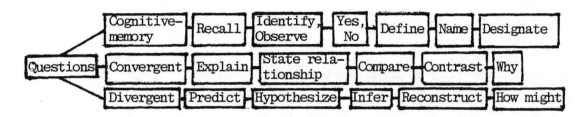

There is one more category to learn. If you have had little difficulty to this point, great! The variety of questions you will ask as a teacher has probably been increased already.

## Evaluative Questions

This category deals with that area of questioning related to judgment, values, and choices. An evaluative question tends to force a student to organize his thoughts and knowledge, to reach a decision, and to take a position which he is willing to justify or to defend. His judgment must be based upon some evidence and standards which he or some other person or group establishes. Questions of this type are often hard to classify properly. Usually evaluative questions call for a response that is neither right nor wrong. The response is an opinion, i.e., Justify your feeling about the President? The following set of questions will provide you with some examples.

Example Questions

    A. Why do you think that modern society tends to undermine family cohesiveness?
    B. Why do you think that John F. Kennedy was a good president?
    C. Do you believe that the volunteer army is better than the draft?
    D. What do you believe should be done to help reduce juvenile delinquency?
    E. What are your reasons for believing that former Vice-President Agnew did not receive a fair trail?

Often evaluative questions are distinguished by short introductory phrases such as:

A. What do you think about. . . ?
B. In your opinion. . . ?
C. Do you believe. . . ?
D. Why do you think. . . ?
E. Justify your belief. . . ?
F. Defend your opinion. . . ?

The wording and the context in which evaluative questions are asked have a significant influence on whether the question actually fits this category or not.

You have five different ways of classifying questions. In the practice below use CM, C, D, E, or N to label each question.

Identification practice (please mark you answers in the space provided)

_____ A. If Napoleon had not been defeated at the Battle of Waterloo, how might the position of France to Europe be different today?
_____ B. What would be the best means of enforcing the anti-pollution laws?
_____ C. What would be your reaction to limiting the size of families by law?
_____ D. In what country is the Black Forest located?
_____ E. In what ways do democratic governments compare?

If you labeled any of these items N, go back and review your mistakes. Only questions B and C should have been marked with the letter E. Question B directs the student to make a choice between alternatives while question C seeks his opinion. The only cognitive-memory item was question D. Students must make a series of comparisons in question E which is one of the cognitive operations called for in convergent questions. Question A should be labeled divergent because the student is asked to hypothesize. If you answered these five questions correctly, you are doing excellent work.

Key words when writing evaluative questions.

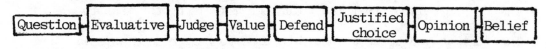

Writing Practice

1.

2.

3.

Where have we been?

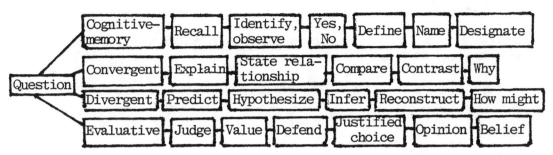

## Summary

Paying attention to the wording of questions is very important. By simply changing a word or a phrase, questions can serve to elicit different cognitive functions. The set of questions which follow illustrate this point.

Cognitive-Memory Questions
A. What is the birth rate in the United States?
B. How many Senators does each state send to Congress?
C. How many degrees north of the equator is New York City?
D. Did William the Conqueror invade England in 1066?

Convergent Questions
A. How does the birth rate of the United States compare to that of France?
B. How does the number of Senators elected from each state compare to the number of Representatives?
C. Compare the cities of New York, Los Angles, and Chicago?
D. Why was William the Conqueror able to invade and conquer England while Hitler could not?

Divergent Questions
A. What would happen to the standard of living in the U.S. if the birth rate increased from 2.1 to 3.0?
B. How might our political system be different if each state elected the same number of Senators and Representatives to Congress?
C. What might happen to New York City if its harbor became silted?
D. Suppose Hitler had conquered England, how might that have changed the course of World War II?

Evaluative Questions
A. What type of action do you think the government should take to reduce the family size of the poor?
B. Do you think the seniority system in Congress is beneficial or a deterent to good government?

   C. Why do you feel that large cities such as New York should be given
      the status of a state?
   D. What are your reasons for thinking that Hitler should have attempted
      to conquer Great Britain before he invaded Russia?

Writing Practice

   It is your turn again. Try taking a single topic and writing one
question representing each category. Once again, space has been provided
below.

   1.

   2.

   3.

   4.

## Applying the Four Types of Questions

   Having read this chapter on questioning, you now know the difference
between the four basic types of questions that are normally asked in the
classroom. Educators know something about the kinds of questions teachers
ask. An analysis of social studies textbooks made some years ago revealed
that approximately ninety-five percent of all questions asked in the text
were cognitive-memory or convergent. Similar studies have been run on
teachers' questions in the classroom. It isn't surprising that ninety
percent of all questions teachers ask are cognitive-memory or convergent.
In other words, social studies teachers have a strong tendency to ask students to recall information either verbatim (cognitive-memory) or in their
words (convergent). But in either case the results are approximately the
same, that is students believe that social studies is primarily the recalling, recitation of content. Needless to say, a pattern of questioning
which only requires cognitive-memory or convergent thinking will not
ordinarily encourage higher level thinking.

## Use All Four Levels.

   What questioning strategy will encourage all levels of thinking? The
answer to this question is very simple and direct. Discussion is stimulated
by the use of all four types of questions. You can't get people to give
thoughtful responses just by asking them to recall, nor are you likely to
generate thoughtful response just by asking evaluative questions. It's

equally important to speculate (divergent) as it is to recall information
in one's own words (convergent). It is the accumulated effect of having
people evaluate, speculate, recall and recite that is most likely to excite
the students' imagination. Some teachers choose to start a discussion with
cognitive-memory and proceed methodically to convergent, divergent, and
evaluative in that order. Others choose to do it in the reverse. Frankly,
what evidence we have suggests that there is no one best way to start. The
only important part of the strategy is that all four questions be asked.

## Motivation

We need to discuss a very practical problem. Many teachers say that
they cannot get their students to answer questions. The students just
won't talk. It's probably true that a certain portion of the class, for
whatever reason, will not respond. Think a minute about the opening remarks
above about the types of questions that teachers and texts ask. You might
agree that there is a considerable amount of monotony in asking only cognitive-memory and convergent questions. The students say they're bored,
maybe to a point they are. After all, there is an appearance of sameness
if day after day the level of questioning in class is at only one level.
Asking the same kind of questions may lead to student apathy, they just
don't want to volunteer anymore. And finally, what is there to discuss about
a recall answer? From the students' point of view the teacher lectures or
gives information as an addition to the students' response. This teaching
strategy (recitation, lecture) as studies show, does not stimulate students
to think for themselves. Frankly, the recitation and lecture, which seems
to be most popular with social studies teachers, tends to turn off discussion
and willingness to participate. That's hard to accept, but it's true.

## Different Level Questions for Different Students

Not surprisingly different students seem to respond to different types
of questions. Some students are perfectly happy answering cognitive-
memory and convergent questions. Others seem to respond better to evaluative and even questions that ask for speculation. When this is pointed out,
teachers are quick to say, "You mean the bright students will answer the
speculative and evaluative and my slower students respond to recall."
That's not true. Students who have great difficulty recalling specific
information might have something to contribute in the form of evaluations,

whereas some of the brighter students pick up information easily and recite it but do not respond well to speculating about it. It is true that concrete experiences tend to be appropriate for the slower students, but that does not mean that they will not respond to questioning beyond the recall level. "Well," teachers will say, "that sounds nice, but I tried that strategy last week and it didn't work, just can't get them to do anything more than sit there. They just want to know what's going to be on the test." We all understand for we all have experienced classes that haven't wanted to participate. The only answer is that you must give all four levels of questioning a chance. This includes asking all four levels on your tests. Students will not respond to a variety of levels in class if your tests are only one level. It takes time to recondition the students to multi-level questioning strategy. The exchange of ideas at different levels seems to stimulate students to a greater desire to participate. One day, one week, perhaps one month, is not going to make a great difference. Very possibly one semester will.

## Applying the Inquiry Method

An inquiry questioning strategy is an absolute necessity if you are going to apply the method. That strategy is not terribly hard, it merely requires that you ask all four different types of questions. The pattern of questioning that you follow is governed primarily by the type of class that you teach. It is not required that you ask more evaluative questions than you would cognitive-memory, nor should they all be equally asked so that a quarter of the class time is devoted to each. One type of question should lead to another. An evaluative should lead to some call for evidence, cognitive-memory or convergent. It is important that a line of thinking be pursued, probed, analyzed, synthesized, and evaluated. Different students respond to different types of questions. It is your task as a teacher to discover which questions your students respond to. Now that you know the four different types of questions, it is appropriate that you be asked to try a strategy that requires the skill of asking the four different types of questions.

## Your Attitude Toward the Four Types of Questions

I wonder how you personally feel about the four types of questions.

Yes, you did learn the difference between the four and noted the argument that you should apply all four types of questions in the classroom, but yet you haven't had the opportunity to identify your preferences. Do you have a preference for one type of question over another? What is your attitude toward the four types of questions? I think it is possible to identify your preference and attitude if you fill out the Question Inventory below.

Instructions:

I. Preference: For each group of questions below, tell which one you would most like to ask by placing a "1" in front of it, a "2" in front of the next, a "3" in front of the next and a "4" in front of the question that you are least interested in.

II. Strength of Choice: After each of the questions below, circle how you feel about that question as follows: A=strongly like, B=like, C=neutral, D= dislike, E=strongly dislike.

After you have ranked preference and strength of choice, use the guide following to mark each of the questions in the four sets either CM, C, D, or E so that you can know the type of question you have ranked.

use this column only after ranking: type of question

| type of question | Rank | | | strongly like | like | neutral | dislike | strongly dislike |
|---|---|---|---|---|---|---|---|---|
| | | (example) | | | | | | |
| E | 4 | 1. | How do you feel about. . . . | A | B | C | (D) | E |
| CM | 2 | 2. | When was the first. . . . | A | (B) | C | D | E |
| C | 1 | 3. | What is your. . . . | A | (B) | C | D | E |
| E | 3 | 4. | In your opinion. . . . | A | B | (C) | D | E |
| ___ | ___ | 1. | Why did the. . . . | A | B | C | D | E |
| ___ | ___ | 2. | In your opinion. . . . | A | B | C | D | E |
| ___ | ___ | 3. | Describe the. . . . | A | B | C | D | E |
| ___ | ___ | 4. | What would happen. . . . | A | B | C | D | E |
| ___ | ___ | 1. | What would you predict. . . . | A | B | C | D | E |
| ___ | ___ | 2. | When did. . . . | A | B | C | D | E |
| ___ | ___ | 3. | Do you believe. . . . | A | B | C | D | E |
| ___ | ___ | 4. | Explain how this. . . . | A | B | C | D | E |

| | | | | | | | |
|---|---|---|---|---|---|---|---|
| _____ | _____ | 1. What do you think about. . . . | A | B | C | D | E |
| _____ | _____ | 2. What would it be like if. . . . | A | B | C | D | E |
| _____ | _____ | 3. How are they similar. . . . | A | B | C | D | E |
| _____ | _____ | 4. Identify the. . . . | A | B | C | D | E |
| _____ | _____ | 1. Name the. . . . | A | B | C | D | E |
| _____ | _____ | 2. Compare the. . . . | A | B | C | D | E |
| _____ | _____ | 3. Suppose the. . . . . | A | B | C | D | E |
| _____ | _____ | 4. Why do you think. . . . | A | B | C | D | E |

Key to type of questions:

| | |
|---|---|
| C | 1. |
| E | 2. |
| CM | 3. |
| D | 4. |
| D | 1. |
| CM | 2. |
| E | 3. |
| C | 4. |
| E | 1. |
| D | 2. |
| C | 3. |
| CM | 4. |
| CM | 1. |
| C | 2. |
| D | 3. |
| E | 4. |

Totals:
Remember, the lower the total, the greater your preference for that type question.

CM _____

C _____

D _____

E _____

Interpreting your Response

This inventory was originally developed for a ESEA Title IV-C research project of the North Montgomery Community School Corporation. The form was administered to hundreds of students, elementary and secondary with the expectation of measuring their preference and strength of choice toward the four types of questions. Many classroom teachers have maintained that students prefer cognitive-memory and convergent type questions. Students responding to this form generally favored divergent and evaluative type questions which is a direct contradiction to the beliefs of many teachers.

How did you respond? Inspect the preference side (left side) of the form. Remember you ranked your preference with one being the highest and four the lowest. From each group of questions add the preference ranks for each level. For example, suppose you marked the divergent question second in the first set of questions, third in the second set, first in the third set, and second in the fourth set. The total would be eight. The lower the total number, the greater your preference for that type of question. Now for strength of choice, in other words, your attitude toward the different types of questions. Perhaps all you need to do at this time is to look at your positive, neutral, or negative feelings toward certain types of questions. If you do have negative feelings toward certain types of questions, do you think that feeling will be reflected in your classroom teaching? Is it possible you might have to change your attitude if you are to use all four types of questions? Finally, your attitude toward questioning is undoubtedly the most important attitude in the class. Whether students think at all four levels in your class depends almost entirely on you.


## SELF TEST

Here is a final check on how well you can classify questions using the four categories you have just learned. Answer all the items. If you are unsure about any of them, refer to the completed chart. Use the letters CM, C, D, and E. When you have finished, turn to the last page and check your answers. Please use the appropriate following work sheet to respond to the questions.

1. What will happen to the U.S. economy if there is a major shift to the production of compact cars rather than big cars by the automobile industry?
2. What do you predict will be the position of the U.S. as a world power in the year 2000?
3. In your judgment, who makes the greater contribution to society, a doctor or a lawyer?
4. What are the similarities and differences between tribes of East and West Africa?
5. When did Texas join the Union?
6. What are the similarities and differences between the concepts of "status" and "role"?
7. How do the administrations of Nixon and Harding compare and contrast?
8. What is the best way to combat inflation?
9. As the Prime Minister of India, how would you insure that everyone received an education?
10. What is the relationship between the production of goods and the standard of living?
11. Who was the last Stuart King of England?
12. What steps would you take to insure that each citizen pays his or her equitable share of income tax?

13. Defend your reasons for deciding to live in the city?
14. If given a choice, would you rather have freedom or security?
15. What is the name of the highest mountain in the world?
16. How are countries in the middle latitudes north and south of the equator alike and/or different?
17. How many people live in the Soviet Union?
18. Suppose that marijuana was legalized: what effect might that have on American society?
19. Do you think that a person accused of a mass murder can receive a fair trial?
20. Did Hannibal conquer Rome?
21. Which country was the first to land a man on the moon?
22. Compare the Democrat and Republican parties?
23. How do you feel about the issue of a guaranteed annual wage?
24. How do you explain the difference between a democratic and socialistic form of government?
25. What inference can you make about life during the reign of William the Conqueror, based on entries in the Doomsday Book?

YOU MAY CHECK YOUR ANSWERS BY REFERRING TO THE KEY ON THE NEXT PAGE.

ANSWER SHEET FOR SELF TEST
ON QUESTIONING SKILLS UNIT

1. _____     6. _____     11. _____     16. _____     21. _____

2. _____     7. _____     12. _____     17. _____     22. _____

3. _____     8. _____     13. _____     18. _____     23. _____

4. _____     9. _____     14. _____     19. _____     24. _____

5. _____     10. _____     15. _____     20. _____     25. _____

## SCORE

23-25     Excellent.  You have mastered all four categories very well.

20-22     Good.  Although you missed a few, your working knowledge is above average.

16-19     Take a close look at those you missed.  It may be that you are slightly confused on one of the categories.

0-15      Check the description of each category carefully and try to determine exactly why you made so many mistakes.

## ANSWER KEY

| | | | | | | | | | |
|---|---|---|---|---|---|---|---|---|---|
| 1. | D | 6. | C | 11. | CM | 16. | C | 21. | CM |
| 2. | D | 7. | C | 12. | D | 17. | CM | 22. | C |
| 3. | E | 8. | E | 13. | E | 18. | D | 23. | E |
| 4. | C | 9. | D | 14. | E | 19. | E | 24. | C |
| 5. | CM | 10. | C | 15. | CM | 20. | CM | 25. | D |

PART II:   UNIT 9

## SKILL DEVELOPMENT IN THE SOCIAL STUDIES
Sheila Wineman and Jacquelin Stitt

Process skills are the skills (or procedures) we use to process information when we think through problems and make decisions.  Some of the process
skills which can be developed and refined through social studies experiences
are:

1.  analyzing — separation of a thing into its parts or elements to
    find out what it's made of; care examination.

2.  classifying -- arranging or grouping according to class or kind.

3.  communicating -- to give information by talking, writing, etc.;
    to convey a message clearly.

4.  comparing and contrasting -- carefully examining the similarities
    and differences of two or more objects, ideas, etc.

5.  defining -- stating the meaning of; describe; explain.

6.  describing -- telling in words what something or somebody is like;
    a word picture.

7.  evaluating -- determining the value and/or accuracy of an idea,
    product, plan, etc.

8.  experimenting -- a trial or test undertaken to discover something
    new or whether something is true; to make tests to find out something.

9.  generalizing -- drawing a general conclusion from a number of parti-
    cular instances or happenings; to infer something from a number of
    particular cases.

10. hypothesizing -- making logical guesses about what will happen in
    an experiment or problem situation; a tentative explanation.

11. inferring -- translating and gaining a basic understanding of the
    material or situation, and expanding beyond this information; a con-
    clusion reached by reasoning.

12. interpreting -- to bring out the meaning of or give special meaning
    to (as in one's own interpretation of something).

13. <u>observing</u> -- watching, seeing, noticing carefully; the ability to examine with exactness.

14. <u>planning</u> -- working out a course of action beforehand; developing a scheme for making, doing, or arranging something.

Although the responsibility for developing these skills crosses all subject area lines, the social studies teacher should make a concerted effort to plan for their development, refinement, and practice. The following section provides a more detailed explanation of why process skills are important, followed by an examination of a procedure which may be used to insure student involvement with these skills.

## Why is Process Skill Development Important?

One purpose of teaching social studies is to acquaint students with their world (past, present and future) and to help them acquire the skills necessary to live in their world successfully. <u>What</u> we present in social studies (the content) will determine how well acquainted the students are with their world (how it was, how it is today, and what it can be in the future). <u>How</u> we present this content can have a direct influence on the development and refinement of the skills which can add to the success of their daily living. We refer to these skills as <u>process</u> <u>skills</u>.

A content analysis can aid us in determining <u>what</u> we will teach, since it enables us to identify the facts, concepts, and generalizations related to a chosen topic of study. However, to complete the planning process, we must also decide <u>how</u> the students will achieve understanding of this content. Some useful questions to ask in making this "how" decision are:

1. Exactly <u>what</u> would I like the student to learn, based on my analysis of the content?

2. Considering where my students are in the development of their process skills and considering the content to be explored, what would be the best teaching method or methods to use? The transmission method? Inquiry? A combination?

3. Based on the method or methods identified, what specific experiences can I provide which will involve students with the content, as well as develop and refine their process skills?

4.   What specific process skills will the students use as they go
     through these learning experiences?

We can view the answering of these questions as a process analysis, since we
are  led to decisions as to how we'll present the content and how the students
will learn it (i.e., what process skills they'll use to achieve understanding
of the content).  Let's take a closer look at these questions and some examples related to each.

1.   What would I like the students to learn, based on my analysis of the
     content?  Let's assume that your students have expressed an interest
     in the problems and needs of the elderly because of recent media
     coverage.  You also feel this is a worthy topic for study and pro-
     ceed to gather background information, resources, materials, and
     media to develop a unit on the topic.  You do a content analysis on
     the information you've gathered and identify all of the facts, con-
     cepts, and generalizations toward which the activities and experi-
     ences in your unit will be directed.  (If you'd like to review the
     process involved in content analysis, refer to Part II, Unit 1,
     "Definitions and Examples of Facts, Concepts, and Generalizations.")
     For our purposes, let's assume that one of the generalizations you'd
     like the students to explore is — "Aging is a natural process."

2.   Considering where your students are in the development of their pro-
     cess skills and considering the content to be explored, what would
     be the best teaching method or methods to use?  In analyzing where
     your students are in the development of their process skills, you
     review the previous learning experiences which have been provided
     and the skills which have been practiced and evaluated.  You decide
     that the "skills focus" of this unit on the elderly should be on
     those skills practiced in inquiry and problem-solving experiences.
     You realize, however, that your students cannot take a "steady diet"
     of inquiry, so you make a note to include other kinds of experiences
     as well.  Based on a quick review of the facts, concepts and generali-
     zations you have identified and the resources, media and materials
     which can be used to present these content elements, you make a defi-
     nite decision to use inquiry as your primary teaching method.  After
     all, you've discovered some great ideas for inquiry experiences in

some of the articles and other materials on conditions in nursing homes, medical care costs, leisure-time activities for the elderly, etc., so why not use them? But what about that generalization, "Aging is a natural process?" You really would like for your students to have some common understandings about it and be able to apply these learnings to themselves and their families. What about calling in that physician friend whose specialty is geriatrics and who does an excellent presentation on the aging process and diseases common to the elderly? Such a presentation would provide the facts related to the aging process as well as add variety to the unit activities.

3. Based on the teaching method or methods identified, what specific experiences can I provide which will involve students with the content as well as develop and refine their process skills? Since you have identified inquiry as your primary teaching method, you now proceed to develop inquiry experiences which will involve students in problem situations related to the elderly. One of your inquiry experiences might focus on the concept of mandatory retirement. You might have two people come into the classroom and role-play 65-year-old women, one of which is healthy and energetic, and another who is ill and in need of medical help. The two role-players could explain that they're being forced to retire, describe the extreme difficulties this will cause, and ask the class to decide if mandatory retirement is fair. After defining the specific problem, the class members could break into small groups, develop and test their hypotheses, and share their conclusions in a total group session. The special care needed by some elderly people could be the basis for another inquiry experience. The students could be asked to pretend that their grandfather has been living with them for some time, but it has become almost impossible for the family members to care for him (i.e., preparing and helping him eat special meals, helping him in and out of his wheelchair, giving him his medication, providing entertainment, etc.) Something must be done and their task is to find a solution which would be acceptable to all concerned. Experiences such as these would certainly involve the students with the content and insure the use of their process skills.

4. <u>What specific process skills will the students use as they go
through these learning experiences?</u> If you re-examine the inquiry
experience focusing on mandatory retirement, you find that the
students would be <u>observing</u> and <u>analyzing</u> the role-playing situation.
They would be involved in additional <u>analyzing</u>, as well as <u>defining</u>
and <u>communicating</u> as they define the specific problem to be explored.
The development of their hypotheses would obviously involve them in
<u>hypothesizing</u>, and, depending on the type of research they do in
testing their hypotheses, they would probably be involved in
<u>planning</u>, <u>analyzing</u>, <u>describing</u>, <u>communicating</u>, <u>interpreting</u>, and
<u>evaluating</u>. In developing and sharing their conclusions, the process
skills practiced would probably include <u>planning</u>, <u>inferring</u>, <u>gener-
alizing</u>, <u>evaluating</u>, and <u>communicating</u>. The inquiry experience related to special care needed by elderly people would provide similar
opportunities for the development and refinement of these process
skills. The physician's presentation on the aging process, depending
on the <u>degree</u> <u>of</u> student involvement, could involve the students in
<u>observing</u>, <u>interpreting</u>, <u>analyzing</u>, <u>comparing</u> <u>and</u> <u>contrasting</u>, and
<u>communicating</u>.

PART TWO:  UNIT:  9

SKILL DEVELOPMENT IN SOCIAL STUDIES

## Summary

In this chapter, process skills have been defined, a rationale as well as sample strategies for their development has been given.  It becomes the teacher's responsibility to provide experiences wherein the students have ample opportunity to develop and refine the process skills.  While the examples given illustrated how these skills can be practiced through inquiry, it should be noted that other teaching methods can promote the development of these process skills.

In order to have a clearer understanding of how process skill development can be fostered through the different methods, review the chapters describing the transmission method, the problem-solving method, and problem-solving through inquiry, noting the sample activities included.  Consult the list of process skills at the beginning of this chapter and list the process skills that could be developed through each method.

PART II: UNIT 10

TECHNIQUES FOR INDIVIDUALIZING INSTRUCTION
Jacquelin Stitt and Sheila Wineman

Individualization is a term that refers to the idea of determining the strengths and weaknesses of each student in the class and specifying learning experiences to meet the student's needs. While this is a popular notion, it is a frightening prospect for many teachers. Elementary teachers are responsible for a minimum of five disciplines: language arts, mathematics, science, social studies, and health. Secondary teachers may only have responsibility for one discipline, but with at least five classes per day, they encounter 125-150 students each day. With numbers like this, the fear that teachers feel when individualization is mentioned, is quite understandable.

However, teachers do realize that students are different. To illustrate this point, consider the varying reading abilities present in a typical class. A simple mathematical computation demonstrates the range of reading abilities in the average class. The formula to use is grade level plus or minus the chronological age divided by three ($GL \pm \frac{CA}{3}$). The number yielded is the range of reading grade levels found in the typical class at that grade level. Other ways students may differ include skills and abilities, (e.g., problem solving, etc.) interest, background experience, motivation and learning style (e.g., auditory, visual, kinesthetic, etc.). In individualization, the social studies teacher attempts to respond to these differences among students, while still leading them to facts, concepts, generalizations, skills and attitudes.

In social studies there are certain objectives, both cognitive and affective, that a teacher endeavors to meet. The cognitive objectives reflect the concepts identified in the content analysis and/or the skills the students need to reach the concepts; the affective objectives reflect the attitudes to be developed in the students as a result of their study. Sometimes these objectives are identified in the textbook or in the curriculum guide. Regardless of the source of these objectives, the teacher must decide on the appropriateness of each objective for the students within the class. Because of the differences among students, objectives may be appropriate for some in the class, while unacceptable or unnecessary for others. Thus, the need for individualization.

Individualization may take a variety of forms.  These include grouping, whole class and/or one-to-one learning experiences.  The chart entitled "Grouping Patterns" has been provided to identify the various grouping patterns, including the purposes, advantages, and disadvantages of each.

The grouping pattern(s) that the teacher chooses is the result of careful thought.  The teacher uses available diagnostic information (or gathers his/her own diagnostic information), reviews instructional goals, considers the content to be covered or uncovered, identifies the resources available and process skills required.  After weighing each of these areas, the teacher selects the optimum grouping pattern(s) for use with his/her class at this particular point in time.

The grouping patterns listed here may be used to facilitate individualization that leads to mastery of the objectives.  For example, if the topic of study is "The Westward Movement," grouping may be used to increase students' understanding of concepts, enhance their research skills and promote appreciation for research as a continually valuable learning tool.  To illustrate this, the authors have identified one cognitive objective and one affective objective, the grouping patterns that could be used, and the prescriptive uses of each.

114

## GROUPING PATTERNS

| Group | Purposes | Advantages | Disadvantages |
|---|---|---|---|
| Total Group | Provide experiences needed by everyone; provides an opportunity for sharing of information gained through small group activities. | Provides a common experience designed to enhance the learning of all involved. | May not meet the individual needs of students. |
| Reading Level Group | Study of content in books of differing levels, so that each student can succeed. | Materials suited to students' instructional level; students can acquire skills at the level of competence of each. | Students may feel stigmatized if in low group. |
| Need Group | Follow-up to give specific instruction for an observed skill deficiency. | Adds to pertinence of instruction to fit it to students' needs. | |
| Research Group | Investigation into aspects of subjects to supplement basic textbook materials. | Gives practice and application in reading/study skills; leads to independence of study. | |
| Interest Group | Expand student interest through opportunity to investigate additional information. | Gives practice and application skills; motivates by giving opportunity to develop own interest. | If used at all times, may impede balanced acquaintance with a subject. |

GROUPING PATTERNS, cont'd

| Group | Purposes | Advantages | Disadvantages |
|---|---|---|---|
| Social Group | All students to work on specific topics with peers of their choice. | Motivates the students. | May not give students the opportunity to work with a wide number of their peers. |
| Guidance Group | Allow culturally and socially different students to work together in order to foster greater social development and tolerance. | Brings about opportunity for experience in working with students of dissimilar interests, ability and competence. | Depending upon student understanding, such grouping may prove to be negative in results. |

| Objective | Grouping Pattern | Prescriptive Uses |
|---|---|---|
| Given 12 sample items from the early West, the students will be able to identify the purpose and present adaptation of at least 8. (cognitive objective) | Research Group | After establishing the time period with the class and providing background information, divide the class into 6 groups. Each group is then responsible for identifying the purpose and present adaptation of 2 items. |
| | Whole Class | After the research has been completed, the students from each group share their findings with the whole class in the most creative way possible. |
| The students will be able to derive satisfaction from gaining information through research, as evidenced by a willingness to participate. (affective objective) | Research Group | Each group member makes his/her contribution to the research group and in the whole group presentation. |

In conjunction with identifying the best grouping pattern for achieving each objective, the teacher may want to vary in- and out-of-class experiences, based upon the differences among the students. The chart below describes some of the differences that are found among students and possible teacher responses in individualizing instruction.

| Differences Among Students | Teacher Responses |
| --- | --- |
| Rate Variations | Vary time to complete the assignment; vary the length of the assignment. |
| Reading Abilities | Provide materials at differing reading levels; read the materials to the students; prepare the students for a reading assignment; develop students' vocabulary; utilize study guides to lead the students through the reading assignment. |
| Background Experiences | Provide instructional experiences requiring varying degrees of experience; use pre-reading assistance devices as necessary; introduce vocabulary. |
| Interest | Introduce the area of study by stimulating interest in a topic or by renewing interest in a topic; provide tasks that respond to the varying interests of the students, e.g., music, reading, automobiles. |
| Motivation | Build in extrinsic motivation through positive feedback or instrinsic motivation that allows the child to see his/her learning. |
| Learning Style | Provide instruction on the same topic through reading, viewing, listening and doing. |
| Thinking Skills | Present tasks requiring thought at the literal, interpretive or applicative levels. |

It is also essential to remember that not all students can best demonstrate their learning in the same manner. Some possible ways of evoking student response are:

| | | |
|---|---|---|
| Puppetry | Meeting of the minds | Tape-recording |
| Sketches | Collages | Write a story/song |
| Model | Riddles | Diary |
| Diorama | Maps, graphs, tables | Create another experiment |
| Sand or clay sculpture | Twenty Questions | Make a center |
| Roving reporter | Relief maps | Bring in resource |
| Playwrite | Paper mache' | Teach someone else |
| Videotape | Improvisation | Make a newspaper |
| 60 Minutes report | Mural | Make a comic strip |
| Pantomime | Make a commercial | Cooking |
| Charades | Make a display | Recipes |
| "You Were There" | Shadow Box | Menus |
| Dance | Student developed | Lists |
| Role Play | handouts | Make a book |
| Sing | Flannel board | Collect resource books |
| Rhythm instruments | Radio program | Pack a suitcase |
| Costume | Interview | Sketches |
| Paper sculpture | Share a hobby | Art media |
| Debate | Crossword puzzles | Field trip |
| Games | Story problems | Bulletin board |
| Posters | Word searches | Prepare a handout |
| Make a filmstrip | Write a letter | Slide show |
| Silhouettes | Plan a parade | Teach a lesson |
| Report (oral/written) | Make a movie | Create a flag |
| Mobile | Shadow puppets | Write a newspaper |
| Pencil/paper tests | Coat-of-arms | article |
| Outline | Transparencies | |

A variety of tools can be utilized in individualizing instruction. A chart has been provided describing four of these tools and the pertinent characteristics of each. After reviewing the chart and the samples of each which are available in the clinical laboratory, your assignment is to develop one of these tools.

| Tools | UNIPAC | LEARNING ACTIVITY PACKAGE (LAP) | AUDIO-TUTORIAL LESSONS | LEARNING CENTERS |
|---|---|---|---|---|
| Uses | Teaching Reinforcement in grades | Teaching Reinforcement in grades | Teaching in grades K-12. | Teaching Reinforcement Application in grades K-12 |
| Location and Materials | Teacher distributes to each student to use wherever he/she wishes. All materials necessary are included. | Teacher distributes to each student which he/she may use wherever he/she wishes. Materials are available to the student as he/she needs them. | Tape recorders and the lab packet permit mobility. Necessary materials are on tape or in the lab packet. | All necessary learning materials are located in a designated area: desk, box, bulletin-board, etc. |
| Objectives | Known by the teacher and the student. | Known by the teacher and the student. | Known by the teacher and the student. | Known by teacher |
| Special Characteristics | Pretest used to determine which objectives the students needs to learn more about. | Pretest used to determine which objectives the student needs to learn more about. | Union of the audio and visual modes | Attractive and enticing. Provides opportunities for students to suggest additional activities. |
| Types of Activities | Unipacs given to individuals or small groups.<br><br>Uses a variety of modes<br>Quest activities | Individual; Small groups may be used for discussion. | Individual; Written response could involve the student, following the initial learning. | Individual and small group; Involves a variety of modes; Provide for sharing in different ways with both the teacher and peers. |

| | | | |
|---|---|---|---|
| **Student Evaluation** | Pre- and post-tests as well as self-test. Peer and teacher checking of concept understanding. | Pre- and post-tests Self-correcting activities | Assignments evaluated by the teacher | Individual conferences Total group discussion/sharing of activities completed; Teacher observations; Self-correcting items; Peer checking of concept understanding. |
| **Management** | Pretest results determines activities. Post Test is taken when student is ready, based on self-test. Students can be recycled based on self-test and post-test. | Pretest results determine activities. Post-test is taken when student is ready. Students can be recycled through learning activities if mastery is not demonstrated. | Introduction to A-T lessons. Scheduling time when a student may use the tape recorder. Providing instructions on the appropriate use of the tape recorder. | Contractual agreements; Schedule individual/small groups into the center. Introduction to L.C. Provide direction for: ea. activity, appropriate behavior, placement of finished products, center care. Choosing appropriate location for center. Limit number of activities available to the number of students in a group. |
| **Record-Keeping** | Teacher records pre- and post-test results. | Teacher records pre- and post-test results. | Students record audio-tutorial lessons used. Teacher records evaluation of learning. | Student progress file maintained by each student. Projects completed in learning center may be evaluated jointly by teacher and student. |

PART TWO:  UNIT 11

DEVELOPMENT OF ATTITUDES AND VALUES IN THE SOCIAL STUDIES

Kenneth Craycraft

Values can be defined as beliefs that affect our actions and reactions to
events, passive or active, occurring in our daily lives.  While few people
would violently disagree with the previous, valuing has been and will continue
to be one of the more controversial areas of our curriculum.  Many factions
within our schools and communities view this topic as a "four-letter word."
Coupled with the conservative tenor of our country, the prevalent attitude
seems to be, "leave the teaching of values to the home and church."  Unfortunately,
we cannot turn-on or shut-off our value systems at will.  As long as human beings
interact, regardless of the setting, values are an integral part of that interaction.  For the remainder of this unit, the previous statements concerning
valuing will be explored in four related areas:

(1)  effects on classroom activities

(2)  kinship to decision making

(3)  relating to the three traditions (see Part I, Unit 2)

(4)  practical classroom activities.

Effects on Daily Classroom Activities

The "back to basics" movement has had a tremendous effect on one of the most
frequently used tools by the classroom teacher the textbook.  Individuals, and
groups, want publishers to incorporate materials that emphasize those ideals or
values that made America strong.  These people feel that there are acceptable
values in select content that should be stressed while distracting information
omitted.  This view raises some extremely important questions.  Who do you know
knowledgeable enough to determine what is best for our students?  Would you feel
comfortable in making the final content selection?  Would you feel confident in
making a "correct" decision examining only part of the available information?
Can you think of other societies that have tried this tactic?  Finally, how is
this different from censorship?  Further exploration will be forthcoming in the
decision making segment.

Beyond the textbooks, personal values are reflected each place we look
in our classroom.  When a child walks in the first day, he or she is greeted
with a list of classroom rules and regulations.  In the back of the room is

a picture of George Washington and Abe Lincoln with the U. S. Flag between
the two. The seats are placed in straight rows and each student sits attentively
as the teacher describes how many recesses will be missed for unacceptable
behavior. In addition, the teacher is very neatly attired with each hair held
in place by "Spray-Net." Smiling is not encouraged as school is a place to
learn - not to have fun. Everyone knows anything pleasurable is sinful.
While the previous is an obvious exaggeration, how many of these examples can
you identify with? What value messages are dictated - without a word being
spoken? Can there then, be a classroom without values? Think about this as
we explore the relationship of valuing to decision making.

## Valuing and Decision Making

As mentioned earlier, proponents of the "back to basics" movement want us
to teach those skills that made us "the greatest nation ever." Their proposed
primary vehicle - the three R's (reading, writing and arithmetic) with social
studies supporting by reviewing dates and events. While no one in their right
mind would question the validity of knowledge in these areas, what is any more
basic than decision making? There is not a day that passes when decisions are
not made. Still, can we make decisions without including our value base? What
a dilemma! We want to prepare our students for a productive life in society,
to be knowledgeable and appreciative, to make sound decisions but - no valuing
please!

The decision-making process can be broken into four basic components.

1) Examining a problem by thinking of several possible solutions.

2) Evaluating the feasibility of each possible solution.

3) Choosing the best alternative.

4) Being able to defend the choice.

At no time in this process are we able to proceed without including values.
Valuing, then, seems to be an inherent part of the school day and social studies
curriculum - like it or not. Simply think of all of the decisions our forefathers
had to make. Are we to ask students to forget about the events that led to the
decisions and simply accept the results? It seems only reasonable to assume
greatness is achieved through carefully thought-out actions, and to relegate
these actions to simple outcome reporting is a gross misjustice to the child
and our forefathers. Is "back to basics" then, a step forward or back? The
decision is yours.

## Valuing and the Three Traditions

As mentioned in Part I: Unit 2, social studies has been historically taught in one of three ways: Citizenship transmission, as a social scientist and through reflective inquiry. This segment will briefly explore the ramifications each tradition has on the teacher's view of valuing.

Should a teacher be an individual that primarily identifies with the citizenship transmission made, inculcation won't be the vehicle from dealing with values. This person has definite ideas of "right" and "wrong" and wants students to reflect his/her thinking. He/she feels life experiences have provided the insight to impart views and opinions as absolutes. "Acceptance" is then the word of the day and the key of dealing with valuing situations. The end product - a citizen that shares identical views - one that will do what he/she is told. What do you see as three strengths and weaknesses of this method?

| Strengths | Weaknesses |
|-----------|------------|
| 1. | 1. |
| 2. | 2. |
| 3. | 3. |

The social scientist's method of dealing with values is one of total impartiality. An individual must collect data, weigh and analyze the evidence and objectively arrive at his/her conclusions. Accordingly, human emotion only fosters indecision and results in a less than desirable decision. In the scientific manner, all truths must be proven before results can be considered factual. This person prides him/herself in conducting a "valueless" classroom. Again, think of the strengths and weaknesses of this view. List three of each.

| Strengths | Weaknesses |
|-----------|------------|
| 1. | 1. |
| 2. | 2. |
| 3. | 3. |

The reflective inquirer views valuing in a totally different perspective than the previous two traditions. This person sees the values individuals have as being more dependent as a situation rather than an absolute unchanging conviction. While basic beliefs will be the "rule of thumb," a person can alter his/her values to accommodate certain circumstances. An example of this

is a person's value of stealing being wrong but not hesitating to take food
to save another's life.  This can be explained in two ways; as a hierarchy of
values in which human life took presidence or that values may be situational.
As you may surmise, simply trying to internalize this can create dilemmas.
Basically though, the inquirer suggests that consequences of behavior be weighed
before actions are taken.  What do you think about this position?

| Strengths | Weaknesses |
|-----------|------------|
| 1. | 1. |
| 2. | 2. |
| 3. | 3. |

## Content Summary

The next, and probably most important question you have is:  What are
my obligations as a classroom teacher?  The first step is to recognize valuing
as an inherent component of each school day.  You may not openly discuss
aspects of valuing but, as has been discussed earlier, it exists just the
same.  Try to foster a more open atmosphere where students are encouraged to
freely discuss their feelings concerning topics of interest - either current
or historical in nature.  Secondly, if you are a primary teacher (K-3) spend time
assisting students in developing a more positive self-concept.  It is too easy
to criticize and label a child as a failure.  The competitive nature of schooling
can strike a devastating blow if you do not accentuate the positive.  A great
deal of what is said about values is ingrained with this age.  To ignore values
and self-concept development will only add to an already confusing environment.

As a teacher of the intermediate or middle school aged child, spend time
incorporating valuing into the decision-making process as an integral portion
of the content.  Decisions should not be made haphazardly and students can be
assisted in this realization if valuing is taught in conjunction with their
exploration of dates, places and events.  Furthermore, better decision-making
skills can be fostered by applying the same process to current concerns of
the students.  Social studies is often boring because relevance is hard to
establish.  Brainstorming, debates, etc. (see Part II, Unit 3) can enhance
interest in any topic.  Furthermore, valuing as it exists within decision making
is reinforced as a process.  This is extremely important as views and beliefs
should be developed after considerable self-evaluation and not on the "spur of
the moment."  What more valuable "basic skill" can be stressed?

Forthcoming are several examples of valuing exercises.  Remember, valuing does not exist as a separate entity, it is in everything we do and a part of everything we are.  Should you decide to develop valuing lessons, each can be easily adapted to the suggested lesson plan format.

Examples of Valuing Activities*

---

*The first four examples are from James Barth.  Elementary and Middle School Social Studies Curriculum Program, Activities and Materials.  (Washington, D. C.:  University Press of America, 1979).  The following five examples are from James Barth.  Advanced Social Studies Education.  (Washington, D.C.: University Press of America, 1977).

## EXAMPLES OF VALUING PROCEDURES

Specific Objective:  Valuing the knowing of oneself (Grade kindergarten).

1.  Activity & Materials

    Put Me Together (valuing the uniqueness of self)

    when:      three weeks

    what:      brown (butcher) paper, masking tape

    how:       Trace around each child naming parts of the body, then
               have child paint or color tracing.  Cut portrait outline
               and then cut into separate body parts (one person at a
               time).  Attach little roles of masking tape to the back
               of each piece.  Have child stand in front of mirror and
               reassemble parts working from head to feet.  Remove tape
               and place pieces in envelope for further practice away
               from mirror.

hair
face
ears
neck
arm
wrist
hand
thumb
fingers
trunk
legs
thigh
calf
ankle
foot
shoe

2.  Activities & Materials

    Me, Myself, and I (valuing the uniqueness of self)

    when:        two weeks

    what:        coat hangers, paper

how:       —make a booklet including sheets for:  my name, my picture,
           my hand, my footprint, my house, my friend, my room, my
           toys, etc.
           —make a mobile using a coat hanger

Specific objective:  Identify actions or feelings that are similar or different
from story book characters.

3.  Activity & materials

        Reactions (valuing feelings)

    when:      recurring

    what:      stories, films, etc.

    how:       read story or show film and ask questions, i.e., "What would
               you have done or felt if 'it' had happened to you?"

               Have children draw pictures about what they liked best and
               then let child dictate sentences about drawing, i.e., "I
               liked the part where. . ."  Make papers into a book.

4.  Activity & materials

        Feelings (valuing feelings)

    when:      recurring

    what:      stories

    how:       read stories showing emotions (fear, love, etc.)  Choose a
               feeling such as "I felt angry........."  Have children draw
               pictures of themselves in a situation that made them angry
               (friend broke favorite toy, etc.) and then have child dictate

story that goes with picture.  Vary emotions.

Discuss how all people have similar emotions.

Discuss mixed emotions, i.e., want to start kindergarten but afraid to go to school.

Specific objective:  Examining one's own beliefs and values (Grade 4).

1.  Activity & materials

We Like...  (identifying similarities in values and beliefs)

when:    one period

what:

how:    have each student pair with another student who has the same interest (model ship building).  Have them touch in some way (lock elbows, hold hands).  Each pair then tries to join with another pair on another shared interest or an expansion of the earlier one (model building of any kind).  The four lock elbows, hold hands or touch somehow.  The foursomes try to join on a shared interest.  Continue until whole class is one big circle that shares an interest.

2.  Activity & materials

Beliefs  (identifying similarities in values and beliefs)

when:    three or four periods

what:    materials as needed for activity

how:    1) pick a TV show (Grizzley Adams, Gentle Ben) a movie the whole class has seen (Wizard of Oz) or show a movie to class. Discuss one of the major characters in the movie:  what the character did and why, and what beliefs or values the character might hold that would cause the character to act the way he/she did.  Discuss what students would do in a similar situation.  Are there similarities and differences between what they would do and what the character did and what they value as compared with what the character seems to value? 2) clean the toy box:  teacher makes a list of toys and objects that might be stored in a toy box (books, baseball cards, football, skates, clay, ball and jacks, broken alarm

clock, toy telephone, toy cars, trucks, dolls, etc.) Give
each student a copy of the list and have them pick toys
they would discard and tell why. What do the lists reveal
about students' values and beliefs? Are there similar lists
between students?

1. Identifying Current Global Values (Grade 7).

when: two periods

what: newspaper or magazine reports on a country or group of
countries selected by teacher. For example:

Tehran, Iran—Many thousands
of Moslems protested against
the Shah of Iran when they
marched through the streets
of Tehran. The Moslems were
demonstrating their objection
to the Shah's plan to try
Western style democratic
reforms such as extending
voting rights, holding democratic elections and supporting
a representative legislature.
The protesting Moslems favor a
return to strict Islamic rule.

Farnborough, England—Britains
"air and space bazaar" which is
held every two years, opened
Monday with many fewer war
planes from the United States
and none from Russia. Emphasis
is on products manufactured in
Third World countries and on
cooperation between nations on
earth and in space.

how: Examine headlines and major points of stories. What values
are inferred. Using sample news stories above for example:

| Values Inferred | Support for Inference |
| --- | --- |
| Democratic values (Shah) | Proposed reforms |
| Islamic values (protestors) | Protests in the streets |
| Cooperation | Third World products |
| Peaceful use of space and land | Fewer military planes |

Specific objective: Identifying how the values of national leaders effect
decisions in a different time and place.

2.  Activity & materials

> ## Time Machine

when:   one period

what:   chart

how:    Imagine that the following people have been carried through space and in some cases time.  Jimmy Carter finds himself in the Germany of Adolph Hitler.  He is to take the place of Hitler in 1932.  Ghandi is to replace Churchill.  Socrates is to replace Mao Tse-Tung in China.  Attilla the Hun is declared Pope and the Pope is the Soviet Premier in the Kremlin.  Idi Amin is King of the Netherlands; the list, of course, is endless.

What would be the reaction of the above people?  What problems would these men face if they tried to govern using the methods they normally practice?  Use the following chart:

What are the consequences of an individual applying his values and methods in the times to which he is transported?

| Name | Values & Methods | Location to which transported | Time to which transported | Consequences |
|---|---|---|---|---|
| Carter | | Germany | 1932 | |
| Ghandi | | England | 1940 | |
| Socrates | | China | 1977 | |
| Attila | | Italy | 1975 | |
| Pope John Paul I | | Russia | 1978 | |
| Idi Amin | | Netherlands | 1976 | |

Specific objective:  Identifying values from what selected men and women say about each other.

Specific Purpose:  Learning to identify one's own values and beliefs and predicting whether these values will change as one grows older (Grade 8).

1.  Activity & materials

## What Are My Values?

when:   one period

what:   My Values form (below)

how:    1) Have students fill out the values form below.

2) Discuss responses with students letting them give reasons for their choices. Teacher must be sensitive to the fact that some students may not want to share their choices with the class.

   a) How did you arrive at the values you chose as most important?

   b) Did you have a hard time deciding how to answer the items in the future?

   c) Do some people have a hard time deciding what they value?

   d) Are some people afraid to say what they really value and put down what they think others value?

   e) Do you think your values are similar to your parents' values?

## MY VALUES

Check each item in the appropriate space or spaces.

1.  Looks
2.  Good grades
3.  Money for material goods: clothes, car, stereo, etc.
4.  Independence
5.  Religion
6.  Marriage and family
7.  Popularity

| | Present | | | Future | | |
|---|---|---|---|---|---|---|
| | Value Most | Neutral | Value Least | Value Most | Neutral | Value Least |

8. Athletic ability
9. Do what parents·
   expect
10. Be a success in a
    career
11. Have leisure time
12. Create something
    (be creative)
13. Do good for society
14. Set a goal and work
    toward it.

A. Are any of your values going to be difficult to combine?

Examples:  woman with family and career

leisure and successful career

B. What in the future might make it easier to reach goals?

example:  four day work week and leisure

C. Do you think your values will change when you graduate from high school or enter college? _____

If so, how? _____

_____

2. Activity & materials

Keeping the Message Up Front

when:   one period

what:

how:    1) have children write down bumper stickers they see on cars
        and bring them to class.

        2) Write bumper sticker messages on board.  Examples:  "School's
        Open, Drive Carefully;" "I Brake for Animals;" "Hire a Vet;"
        "America, Love It or Leave it;" "Stay off my Case;" "If You Can

Read This, You're Too Close."

3) Discuss messages.  Do they represent any values?  What values?  Can the different messages be classified into categories such as people, places, and things?

4) If possible get a student with a camera or provide a camera to a group who would take slide pictures of bumper stickers.  The task would be to organize the slides to fit certain categories of meaning.  The slide show is particularly effective  in getting the point across that people are trying to deliver a message even if it is only on the back of a car.

Conclusions.  As mentioned earlier, valuing is always present in the classroom and is not an area that can be turned on or off at will.  What it does is pose a challenge to help our students deal with issues not always clear to them.  Also, by utilizing a strategy such as the one given, inculcation is avoided and many resulting negative factors.  Values are not promoted, but rather explored.  They are examined and dealt with.  And, by doing this, we are removing our heads from the sand and hopefully dealing with education as it should be—as an extension of society and the "real world."

PART III:  PUTTING IT ALL TOGETHER OR HOW DO I DO IT?

INTRODUCTION

Planning is like the weather:  everybody talks about it, but there are
not many out there doing much about it.  In Part III, you are instructed
in how to plan units and daily lessons.  You probably will accept this as
a legitimate requirement for successful planning and surely some part of
successful teaching.

But you must sense that there is a difference between the university's
requirements for planning and the real world of the school classroom.  On
the one hand you will be told you must learn to organize, to plan in large
blocks of time, and to break those large blocks into daily lesson plans.  Yet
during field experiences the teachers with whom you come in contact may not
have done the type of unit and lesson planning that the university requires.
In other words, teachers in the "real world" of the public school classroom
may not necessarily plan as you have been instructed.

You should be asking about now, "Why shouldn't I plan as do the professional
teachers in the schools?"  In part the answer is that the experienced teacher
knows the students and has taught the content, and probably the most significant
reason is that the textbooks are the source of planning and organization.
Obviously when you start teaching you will not know your students, the content,
or the text.  You will only know those things after you have actually begun
your teaching career.  As a beginning teacher, do not be discouraged from
planning because some of the "old timers" do not.  Old timers do plan, but in
their own way.

Part III offers you the instruction in planning you will need to be
a successful beginning teacher.  The authors provide unit and daily lesson plan
outlines illustrated with examples.  Part III also includes a valuable unit on
the evaluation of social studies materials.  This unit focuses on the proper
selection of content by showing how to conduct a careful analysis of curriculum
materials.  In the final three units of Part III, we will be dealing with
students who at times have been neglected or misunderstood in the social studies
classroom.  We propose there are techniques and methods of instruction with
which you are familiar that are appropriate when working with these students.  You
will be exposed to definitions and characteristics of the gifted learner,
techniques you can use when a mainstreamed student has been placed in your

classroom, and concepts related to multicultural and global education.

Having read Parts I and II, you have considered what social studies is and how to teach it.  Now we invite you to learn how to "Put It All Together" through planning.

PART III:  UNIT 1

PLANNING SOCIAL STUDIES INSTRUCTION

Larry D. Wills

Have you ever had a college professor who was an expert on a particular subject and lectured the entire period?  It is true that many teachers know their subject matter and yet have difficulty passing their knowledge on to students.  Can you remember a high school teacher you may have had in the past who seemed unorganized and whose subject you did not like—and your grade showed it?

What you are going to do in this chapter is learn how to plan the teaching of social studies in the most effective way.  You know your subject matter, but how do you begin to organize and present it to your students?

Before an individual can expect to experience success in the teaching of social studies or any other area of the curriculum, for that matter, one has to be well-prepared and organized.  The purpose of this chapter is to explain the format and nature of developing units and daily lesson plans for instruction in the area of social studies.

## THE UNIT PLAN

First, let's define our terms.  A unit is an idea or topic that usually requires three or four days to maybe four weeks to complete.  Examples of possible units might include "The Presidency,"  "The Civil War,"  "Juvenile Delinquency,"  "Modern Japan," or "The American Indian."  Once the unit topic has been selected, it is necessary to begin planning its introduction to culminating exercises in an effort to secure a proper sequence of activities and meaningful learning experiences for the student.

The first step in constructing the unit should be the creation of a working outline.  This will include major facts, concepts, and generalizations to be covered.  Also, it should provide an opportunity to divide the topic into logical sub-components (i.e., topic,: pollution with sub-components: air, ground, noise, and water).  Following these steps, survey the available materials and make a list of those needed for unit development.  Doing this early will afford the opportunity to acquire those sources of information not readily available to the teacher.

Next, organize the information to this point in a sequential manner and think of ways to secure proper transition from one section to the other. Also, include a variety of learning activities to arouse and heighten student interest in your endeavor. Share what has been done with the instructor or a friend to see whether it makes "sense." Once the above steps have been completed, all that remains is to place the information in a proper unit format.

### Summary

Unit planning has emerged over the last twenty years as a popular way to organize specific topics for instructional purposes. Though there is no one way to construct unit or lesson plans, your instructor may prefer a particular model. In the next section of this chapter you will find various approaches or models of unit and lesson plans.

## DAILY LESSON PLANS

Daily lesson plans are short term plans made each day outlining specifically what and how you are going to achieve for a particular day. In a unit plan general objectives are stated in terms of knowledge, skills, and attitudes/values. The unit plan enables you to organize your activities in broad, global perspectives. The lesson plans enable you to take those general objectives and transform them into specific objectives. In other words you make your unit plan first and then you devise your lesson plans to fit that unit plan. For example, you might have one unit plan and ten lesson plans for a two-week period. If your lesson plans are valid, they will achieve those general objectives contained in your unit plan.

Though you will find various models for lesson plan construction, most models have certain essential ingredients. First there should be clearly stated goals or instructional objectives that should be achieved for a particular day. Second, there should be an outline of instructional activities which you as the teacher will use so that the students can achieve those objectives. These activities might include such techniques as role playing, reading a passage from the text, answering questions asked by the teacher, classroom discussion, playing a simulation game, or viewing a film. All of these are teacher-designed techniques to enable your students to come in contact with content.

138

Throughout your lesson plans, you will need some form of evaluation to determine whether in fact your students are achieving your objectives. Though every lesson plan will not contain some form of formal evaluation, you must always remember that there is a need for some kind of checkpoint to determine whether you and your students are on track and that the students' activities do have meaning. Activity for the sake of activity is mindless, and there should be some reason for all classroom activity. Formal and informal evaluation of student learning will enable you and your students to assess the kind of learning taking place.

In sum, unit and lesson planning are most important for effective classroom instruction, and some of the benefits to you as a teacher can be outlined as follows:

1. When you have a well-planned unit and a series of lesson plans, there is an increased feeling of self-confidence. You know you are prepared, and your students can sense it. From our own experiences, there is less student confusion when you know what you are doing and where you are going. This tends to cut down on student behavior problems. You cannot fool your students. They know when you are prepared, and they will respond to you in more positive ways when you exhibit a feeling of purpose and confidence.

2. It has been said that the only way to "cover a textbook" is to sit on it. We do not advocate your going page by page, chapter by chapter, when teaching social studies. Every textbook should be used as a resource, and you will soon discover there are parts of the text you do not feel are important or which do not meet your own instrutional objectives. Remember you are the teacher--the textbook is not. One of your first tasks, as we have pointed out in preceding chapters, is to select content which is meaningful to your students and which meets your instructional objectives. If you do select your content wisely and with a purpose, you can eliminate that which is unimportant and discard those details which are confusing.

3. You have only so much classroom time to spend with your students in social studies, and every minute does count. If you have a well prepared lesson, you can use the classroom time allotted to you in a

more efficient manner.

4. As teachers, we need to find ways of improving our own instructional techniques. We need to know whether we are successful. It is definitely true that everything we try in the classroom does not work. There are days when our lesson plan falls flat, and we wonder why. If we have lesson plans and units developed, we have a basis for reflecting on what we did. We can then begin to modify existing lesson and unit plans, try them out, and if they work, begin to develop our own skills that meet the realistic expectations of the classroom.

5. Finally, carefully constructed lessons and units enable us to evaluate our students more effectively. If we know what we have taught and we have designed an effective teaching strategy, the grades given to students for their work will reflect a realistic appraisal of what was expected and what we in turn can expect of our students. We should not ask students to do anything we have not prepared them to do. If we cannot find where a particular skill was developed in our lesson plans, then we cannot realistically expect our students to be evaluated from those skills.

In the following section, you will find differing examples of unit and lesson plans. You will notice not all units and lesson plans employ the same methodology. Some lessons may emphasize development of attitudes and values, some will be built around discovery while others emphasize the transmission method.

Regardlss of approach taken in the outline of daily lesson and unit plans, there is some consensus on the following points.

For the unit plans:

1. Were understandings, skills, attitudes/values stated?

2. Did initiatory activities provide for stimulating interest in the unit to be studied?

3. Was there a logical progression of developmental and culminating activities?

4. Was a variety of sources and materials provided?

Evaluation for the lesson plans:

1. Were the objectives stated in behavioral terms?

2. Was there a logical sequencing of instructional activities?

3. How did the teacher allow for evaluation of the day's lesson?

4. Did the procedure of the lesson lead to the accomplishment of stated instructional objectives?

5. Were instructional materials and techniques used other than text and lecture?

## CRITERIA FOR EVALUATION OF UNIT

Mere design of lesson and unit plans is not adequate. What looks good on paper may not meet our needs as teachers or students when the lesson is actually presented. The following items may be used to evaluate the unit of instruction after it has been presented to your students:

1. What was the date and location of the unit tried? Who were the students involved?

2. How well did I achieve my goals and/or objectives?

3. How well did the students respond to each activity planned?

4. How well did I help the students understand the big ideas or concepts as a result of the planned activities?

5. How well did I help the students develop their problem-solving skills as a result of the planned activities?

6. Where did the unit need improvement? What were the strengths and weaknesses of the unit? How could I improve the unit?

7. How did the unit provide for practical use of concepts in daily living for the class?

PART III, UNIT 2

Unit and Lesson Plans

Kenneth Craycraft

The purpose of this section is to acquaint you with lesson and unit plans. While the components may be labeled differently than those in the inquiry unit, the principle remains consistent. That being, to involve the student as much as possible is the learning process. Two key terms to keep in mind as you think about planning are sequencing and transition. Sequencing secures proper ordering of material and the transition moves you smoothly through the procedure. While these two concepts may be relatively easy to understand, the mastery is something like learning to drive a standard shift automobile. In other words, practice, thinking and repetition are your best allies. For the remainder of the section we will explore suggested lesson and unit plan formats with explanation and examples of each.

Lesson Plans

Once you have a topic in mind, the first step should be to identify the major points of emphasis. After having accomplished this, arrange the points in a progressive order. This will assist in sequencing, and, also promote a logical approach to the subject. Furthermore, by identifying the major points, a determination can be made on the number of knowledge objectives required (one per point of emphasis) as well as the types of materials needed. At this point, you are ready to explore the procedural components of the lesson plan.

The first procedural component of the lesson plan is motivation or readiness, with the purpose of securing the students' interest (teaching is much easier when your class is listening to you). When deciding on a particular motivational tool or strategy, make sure it is appropriate and will provide for a smooth transition to the next section. Different techniques or tools can be found in Part II, Unit 3.

The second procedural component is the content section. Once you have the students curious about a topic, provide them with the vehicle(s) to satisfy the curiosity. Remember, content comes in many different forms ranging from lecture to survey and from reading to basic research. Too much of any one technique will eventually guarantee boredom.

After a topic has been explored and the information discussed, the students should have the opportunity to associate or synthesize the ideas. This need gives rise to the third component, closure. This section is designed to review what has been learned and how the smaller parts relate to the whole. Usually, this section does not take a great deal of time, but is extremely important. When teaching, never neglect to include this segment.

Lesson plans that end with the previous steps (and some do) omit the fourth component, application. It is generally felt that if a topic is worth teaching, the knowledge should have some long-range value for the student. This section provides them with at least an immediate usage. Activities can range from letters to role play or from murals to a clean-up campaign. Again, you can refer to Part II, Unit 3 for ideas. To assist in further clarifying the previous explanation, the following lesson plan should be carefully examined. In addition a Self-Check Guide is included to assist in the preparation of future plans.

*Note: Throughout the previous, the term daily plan was not used. It is our belief that a plan should represent a complete idea rather than several fragments. In a teaching situation, teach as far as time permits, mark the stopping point and begin there the next class meeting. Finally, if you are to test the students for a grade, create it from your objective list. After all, these are the points stressed.

NAME _____

DATES _____

LESSON PLAN

GRADE _____

PLAN FOR _____

TIME ALLOWANCE _____

## OBJECTIVES

1) Have you included all of the necessary components for a well-written objective?

   a) Have you identified the source of information?
   b) Have you used an action verb?
   c) Have you identified the acceptable performance?

2) Do you have an objective for each major point covered or emphasized in the lesson?

## CONCEPT
### (Social Studies Only)

What is the concept (big idea) to be presented or discovered in the lesson?

## ACTIVITIES (Procedures)

1) Motivation/Readiness                    Time _____

   a) Have you identified or located an appropriate means for introducing the lesson?
   b) Have you assumed too much or too little background on the students' part for this lesson?
   c) Is it appropriate for this age and this topic?
   d) Have you identified appropriate questions?
   e) Transition statement

2) Content                                 Time _____

   a) Have you arranged the materials that add to the students' formal learning in proper sequence?
   b) Are the materials appropriate for your grade level?
   c) Do you understand the materials thoroughly?
   d) Are the materials too text oriented?
   e) Is this a student-centered or teacher-centered approach?
   f) Have you identified appropriate questions?
   g) Transition statement

3) Closure                                 Time _____

   a) What are you doing or having the students do to "sum up" the lesson?
   b) Will your approach offer the students the opportunity to relate the parts of the material?

4) Follow-up Activity or Application

   a) Is a follow-up activity appropriate?
   b) Is your activity an extension of the learning process?
   c) Will the children enjoy this?

## MATERIALS

1) Have you located all of the materials necessary for this lesson? Have you listed them on your plan?

2) Do you understand how to use any audio-visual equipment?

3) Does the equipment work?

4) Are your materials clear and easy to read and/or understand?

## PROCESS SKILLS
### (Social Studies Only)

What problem-solving skills are the students using throughout the lesson?

144

ACTIVITIES (Procedures continued)

SELF-EVALUATION (After the lesson is taught)

1.  How well did I achieve my goals
    (or objectives)?
2.  How well did the students respond to the
    activity?
3.  How well did I help the students to understand
    the concept (big idea) as a result of this
    activity?  (social studies only)
4.  How well did I help the students to develop
    their problem-solving skills as a result of
    the activity?  (social studies only)
5.  What were the strengths of the lesson?
6.  What were the eaknesses of the lesson?
7.  How could I improve the weaknesses?
8.  Did the lesson provide for any practical use
    of concepts in daily living?
    (social studies only)

Sample Lesson Plan

Name: _____

Date: _____

Grade: _____ 5 or 6

Plan For: _____ Social Studies-Hausa Tribe

## OBJECTIVES

After researching the materials relating to the Hausa Tribe (see M.L. 2-7) the students will be able to:

1) point to the location of the tribe on a globe.
2) list three characteristics of their dress.
3) list four of the most common occupations.
4) list at least four tribal customs
5) identify the advanced country influencing the people.
6) list the four natural resources of the country.

## PROCEDURES

### Motivation

Distribute list of commonly used Hausa words (see attached) to each student in class. Divide the class in 4 groups of 6 and instruct them to try to identify at least 7 characteristics of the Hausa Tribe. Questions to assist the students' efforts:

a) Where do you think these people live?
b) Do you think this is a developed country? Why?
c) What kind of occupations do these people seem to have?
d) What kind of religion do you think they have?
e) etc...

After students have been allowed at least 10 minutes to brainstorm, have each group to report their responses. Record on board.

### Content

Ask students if they are positive all of the characteristics are accurate (TRANSITION).

Utilizing the same groups, distribute materials relating to Hausa tribe and instruct students to check to see how many times they were correct, incorrect, or how many new bits of information they found.

Materials should be rotated every 10 minutes to provide students to explore majority of materials.

## MATERIAL LIST

1) Hausa word list (attached)
2) World Book volume H pages 34-47
3) National Geographic, Sept. 1946 pages 78-91.
4) All About Hausa, pages 170-182
5) Atlas & Globe
6) Newsweek, Oct. 1969, pages 15-21.
7) Hausa, Their Dress, Customs, and History. Pages 1-82.
8) Butcher paper for mural. (All of the above located in rear of room.)

Sample Lesson Plan

Name: _____                    Grade: _____

Date: _____                    Plan For: _____

OBJECTIVES            PROCEDURES            MATERIAL LIST

Closure

Review the material by having groups to
report information as either new, correct,
or incorrect. Again, record the responses
on the board.

Application

In the same groups, have students to
represent their view of the Hausa people
by creating a mural (see M. L. 8) focusing
on one of the following:

a) customs
b) dress
c) housing
d) location (geography)

Place finished product on vacant wall.

Material List #1
*COMMONLY USED HAUSA WORDS

| | | |
|---|---|---|
| cotton | goat | onion |
| Sabbath, Friday | God | agreement |
| cheap | house | rainy season |
| trader, market man | desert | a prohibition, law |
| horse | yams | merchant |
| tax | brass, copper | schoolmaster |
| salt | farm | road |
| witchcraft | grandmother | to catch fish |
| aunt | account | umbrella |
| Koran, book | barber | debtor |
| servant | to owe | slavery |
| walled town, city | tent | cheese |
| soil | tax collector | blacksmith |
| teacher, learned man | butter | camel |
| dry season | cow | to sell |
| furnace, clay oven | mosque | to rust |
| mountain | sheep | mother |
| prophet | brother | devil |
| to pray | gold | bargain |
| sin | | |

*Words list adapted from Barry Beyer. Inquiry in the Social Studies Classroom. (Columbus, Ohio: Charles E. Merrill Publishers, 1971).

148

SAMPLE INQUIRY LESSON PLAN

Name: _____

Date: _____

Grade: _____

Plan For: _____

## OBJECTIVES

1. After watching a puppet play depicting a conflict situation, the children will be able to orally and accurately describe the problem to be solved, and in small groups, orally discuss and state a solution to the problem.

2. After stating a solution to the problem, each small group will develop a role-play of their solution for the total group and after discussing each role play, the total group will have a hand to conclude which solution is best.

3. Following a group discussion on cooperation, each child will develop a poster depicting the hypothesis concluded best and including a statement indicating how cooperation can solve problems.

### CONCEPT

Cooperation means working together to solve problems.

## PROCEDURES

1. Motivation-Presentation of the Problem—(Total Group)
Children will view a puppet play involving two puppets, a boy and a girl.

Girl: Bobby, let's watch "Blue Marble" next. It's my favorite show on Saturday morning T.V.

Boy: No, Susan! We're going to watch cartoons next! You know the Road-runner is more fun to watch than that 'ole "Blue Marble!"

Girl: But, Bobby! It's my turn to choose the next show. You chose the last one!

Boy: It's not your turn either, Susan! I get to choose two shows in a row. That's a new rule.

Girl: That's not fair, Bobby! You chose last and we didn't talk about any 'ole rule! It's my turn to choose!

Boy: No! I get to choose!
Girl: No! Me!
Boy: No! Me!

Bobby and Susan wrestle, each saying over and over, "No! It's my turn, my turn, my turn!" The curtain on the puppet stage suddenly closes.

The teacher then summarizes the problem by saying: Bobby and Susan are having a real problem with the TV and which program to watch. Let's see if we can work out a way they could cooperate with each other and solve this problem!

## MATERIAL LIST

puppet stage
boy puppet
girl puppet
poster paper
crayons
pencils

### SKILLS

observation
analysis
deduction
description
inference
interpretation
communication
hypothesizing
planning

SAMPLE INQUIRY LESSON PLAN

Name: _____

Date: _____

Grade: _____

Plan For: _____

OBJECTIVES

PROCEDURES

MATERIAL LIST

2. Body

A. Defining the Problem (Total Group)

Lead the children into a total group discussion by asking:

1. Who were the puppets? Do you think they were related? Why or why not? How do you know?

2. What day of the week was it? How do you know?

3. Which TV programs did Susan and Bobby want to watch?

4. Why couldn't they watch both programs?

5. Whose turn was it to choose? Explain your answer.

6. How do you feel about Bobby's new rule? Was it fair? Why or why not?

7. Is fighting the best way to solve the problem? Why, why not?

After discussing the questions above, help the students define the problem by asking the following questions:

1. What are all the things you can tell me about the problem? Boy and girl, watching TV on Saturday morning, disagreeing on what show to watch.

2. What are some things you think may be true about the problem? Brother and sister, both have favorite shows on at the same time, there's only one TV.

3. What are some things your're not sure about (or don't know in relation to the problem? Whose turn it was to choose the next TV program.

SAMPLE INQUIRY LESSON PLAN

Name: _____

Date: _____

Grade: _____

Plan For: _____

OBJECTIVES

PROCEDURES

MATERIAL LIST

4. What is the exact problem we're going to solve? Bobby and Susan have a problem with their TV viewing and we need to find a way they can cooperate to solve the problem.

B. Developing Hypotheses—Small Group Divide the children into work groups to develop their hypotheses. Based on their discussion about the puppet play and their definition of the problem, the children may hypothesize that:

1. Bobby and Susan could solve their problem by taking turns watching their favorite TV shows.

2. The problem could be solved if Bobby and Susan save their money and buy a second TV.

3. Bobby or Susan could watch their TV show at a friend's home.

C. Testing the Hypotheses—(Small Group) Each small group will test their hypothesis by:

1. Discussing it among themselves and deciding whether it would work in a "real life" situation in their own homes.

2. Preparing a role playing situation in which they re-create the problem and add their solution.

150

SAMPLE INQUIRY LESSON PLAN

Name: _____

Date: _____

Grade: _____

Plan For: _____

| OBJECTIVES | PROCEDURES | MATERIAL LIST |
|---|---|---|

PROCEDURES

3. Closure
Developing and Sharing a Conclusion
(Small group, total group, and individual)

1. Each small group presents their role play to the total group for further testing.

2. The total group discusses which (if any) hypothesis is best and why.

3. The children vote to determine which hypothesis is best.

4. A discussion will follow the voting which will focus on the need to cooperate to solve problems:

Why is your solution better than fighting?

Which solution is most likely to make everybody happy? Fighting or cooperating?

What are other situations at home where cooperation might help to solve a problem?

5. To share the hypothesis voted best, each child will think of a situation at home where cooperation would be helpful and develop a poster to portray the situation. The poster will include a statement or saying to clarify the message. Posters will be displayed on the Social Studies Factline.

## UNIT PLANS

Several times throughout the school year teachers may decide to prepare for a topic that will take anywhere from one to four weeks to complete. A topic of this scope does not readily lend itself to typical or traditional lesson planning procedures as greater consideration must be given to sequencing and outlining. An effort to approach this undertaking from a daily basis will guarantee failure. It would be like building a house without any plans to follow at all. The end results may provide a shell but unlikely to merit any outstanding home nominations. The following outline is designed to assist the teacher in developing a plan of study from the foundation to completion. Explanations are provided for each step to clarify the precedure.

### *Unit Plan Outline

I.  Introduction

    A.  Topic to be taught

    B.  State the age and/or grade level

    C.  Indicate the approximate length of time needed to complete this topic

    D.  Briefly state how this fits in the overall plan (when applicable).

II.  Content Outline

    A.  Outline the major subject matter content (most frequently used or

    B.  Outline a statement of problems to be solved, or

    C.  Outline a series of projects to be completed.

Note: Regardless of the choice you make in this section (A, B, or C), include sub-topics and sub-points in detail. A complete outline here will make the rest of the unit development much easier.

*Adapted from: Methods of Instruction in Social Studies Education by James Barth. (Washington, D. C., University Press of America, 1979.)

III. Objectives-Stated as Knowledge, Skills or Attitudes

    A.   Outline the specific knowledge which students are expected to master (one per sub-point of outline).

    B.   State the specific skills which students will build (research, notetaking, writing, etc.)

    C.   Outline the specific attitudes which students will develop (cooperativeness, open-minded, critical, respect for, appreciation, self-confidence, etc.).

IV. Activities in Which Students Will Engage to Achieve Objectives

    A.   Initiatory Activity

    Describe the initial activity you have in mind to introduce this topic. State in third person as you would on a lesson plan. The more detail you have here the less work that will be involved in developing lesson plans.

    B.   Developmental Activities (content)

    Describe one series of activities per sub-topic on your outline. Make sure what you have planned will promote the achievement of each of your knowledge objectives. Again, the more detail you have here the less required for lesson plan development.

    C.   Culminating Activities

    Describe the activities you have in mind to assist the students in synthesizing, categorizing and utilizing the information that has been presented. A portion of this segment can and should be a portion of the unit evaluation (not necessarily tests exclusively).

V. Materials and Resources

    A.   Locate reading materials, audio-visual aids, materials for demonstration and experimentation which are needed to make the activities most worthwhile.

    B.   Locate and identify types of facilities outside the classroom in the school and community which will be used.

    C.   Locate and identify individuals that will be willing to present or assist in your classroom (include only if you are doing the activities in C & D).

D. When students are to make contacts with persons outside the classroom or are to secure materials, identify procedures to be employed.

VI. Evaluation Procedures

A. Identify the procedures which will be employed to evaluate the effectiveness of the unit.

B. Identify techniques to be used in assisting students to measure their own progress.

C. Identify procedures which you will use to measure student growth in understandings, skills, and attitudes throughout the unit.

## Example of Unit Plan

Note: The following example is considered to be of moderate detail which would require additional work when developing the actual lesson plans in the schools.

## Example Unit

I. Introduction

A. The concept of "Families"

B. First grade level

C. Approximately 7-10 days

D. This topic fits in the overall plan as the family unit is, at this stage, one of the most important influences on the child's life.

II. Content Outline

A. Introduction - The teacher will need copies of school pictures for each child in the class and place these on a bulletin board entitled "I'd Like You to Meet My Family," which is designed to be the starting point of the discussion on family characteristics.

B. Identify "Family"

1) Members

2) Characteristics

3) Postion (age) of members

4) Types of Families

C. Roles (responsibilities) of Family Members

1) Contribution of each member

2) Duties of each member

3) Responsibilities of each member

D. Where Families Live

1) Houses in different places

2) Types of houses

3) Child's home

E. Family Rules

1) Types of family rules

2) Need for family rules

3) Rules in child's family

F. Family Activities

1) Working activities

2) Fun activities

G. Culminating Activities - The students will create their own family albums with pictures of themselves, drawing, other members and immediate family tree.

III. Objectives - <u>Stated as Knowledge, Skills, or Attitudes</u>

Knowledge

A. After viewing pictures of animals and culturally different humans, the students will be able to verbally list two similarities of each group.

B. After hearing the story <u>The Three Bears</u> and discussing the characteristics of the "Bear" family, the students will be able to:

1) Verbally identify the number of members in their families.

2) Write the number of brothers and sisters in their families.

3) Write the age of each family member.

4) Verbally compare the size of their family to others in class.

C. After hearing the story, Me and You, from You and Me (pp. 121, 123, 125) and discussing family responsibilities the students will be able to:

1) Write three contributions by each family member.

2) Write two duties of each member.

3) Illustrate one responsibility of each member (color Picture).

D. After hearing the story, "Your Family," from You and Me (pp. 19-54, 82, 84, 95-100) see pictures of different houses and discussing differences in housing the students will be able to:

1) List two places houses can be located.

2) Identify four types of shelter where families can live.

3) Draw a picture of their dwelling.

E. After hearing the story, "Their Families" from You and Me (pp. 55-68) and discussing types of and need for family rules the students will be able to:

1) List three types of family rules.

2) Write four reasons for family rules.

3) List three of their family rules.

F. After viewing pictures of different activities and discussing activities families participate in, the students will be able to:

1) Illustrate three working activities.

2) Illustrate two family fun activities.

Skill Objectives

A. The students will utilize listening skills, drawing skills and observation skills.

B. The students will utilize fine motor skills by cutting, pasting, etc.

C. The students will utilize basic research skills by asking family members of immediate family tree.

Attitude Objectives

A. The students will develop an appeciation for differences among and between families.

B. The students will develop a positive attitude.

C. The students will have a better understanding for the need of family rules.

D. The students will have a more complete understanding of family rules.

IV. Activities in Which Students Will Engage to Achieve Objectives

A. Initiatory Activity(ies)

The teacher will place a picture of each child on the bulletin board, "I'd Like You to Meet My Family." This, will be the starting point of the discussion on family characteristics. Discussion should center around elements or similarities of school family to their own family. The teacher should also read page 118 from Me and You and You and Me which emphasizes family characteristics. Review materials and content covered.

B. Developmental Activities

1. Identify "Family"

a) Members - Show students several pictures (see M. L. 2) of Animals and Humans that illustrate groups. Lead discussion of how groups with common interests are like families.

b) Characteristics - Read story, The Three Bears, and then discuss differences in family groups noting membership and size.

c) Postion (age) - Follow previous with discussion of age or position of family member.

d) Show pictures of different family compositions (i.e., single parent, traditional, grandparents, etc.) (M. L. 4) and lead children in discussion of different types of families. It should be emphasized that all family types are acceptable without value judgements indirectly making or inferring one as "better."

2. Rules (responsibilities) of Family Members - To achieve each of the sub-points of this section read to the children the story My Responsibilities at Home which describes the duties of a child around his/her dwelling. The follow-up discussion should emphasize roles, contributions, duties and responsibilities of family members. Ask for examples from the children and have each to illustrate through a drawing. Also, have students ask their parents or guardians of rules they may not be aware of.

3. Where Families Live - Read the story Where Families Live to the children which stresses types of dwellings found in U. S. as well as other parts of the world. Follow this with discussion as well as pictures of different types of "homes" (see M. L. 7). The discussion should be designed to make children feel positive about any place they should happen to live. At the end of the lesson the child should draw a picture of where he/she lives and write a short story telling about the "home."

4. Family Rules - Read to the children the story "My Family" from You and Me, which centers around rules in a family. Discuss and review the contents having students provide examples of rules with the need for each. Follow this with a game that has no rules (see M. L. 8) and play until confusion and noise becomes prohibitive. At this point, again, review need for rules. Then have students give an example of a rule they have at home and one that they think they should have.

5. Family Activities - Show the film "Life on a Farm" which highlights the different activities done on a farm. Review the film and have children relate working activities around their homes. In this section group rather than individual endeavors should be stressed. Following this, have children relate fun activities they either do or would like to do with their families.

C.  Culminating Activities - Students should be compiling a notebook called "My Family Album" as the unit progresses.  Included will be personal family tree, pictures, illustrations and stories that have been gathered throughout the unit.

V.  Materials and Resources

1)  Me and You, You and Me, by Charlotte Zolotow.  McMillan Publishing.

2)  Pictures of Animal and Human Groups (Found in resource packet #1).

3)  "The Three Bears" (story found in Fantasy For Children) ed. by R. T. Simms (reading table).

4)  Pictures of different family compositions (found in resource packet #2).

5)  My Responsibilities at Home, by F. D. Koch, Barker Books, Inc.

6)  Where Family Live, by T. R. Veler, Motion Press, Inc.

7)  Pictures of different housing structures (see resource packet #3).

8)  Game of Concentration with no rules (see resource packet #4 with teacher directions and procedures).

9)  Film - "Life on a Farm" by Astro Video.  13 Minutes (in library).

10.  Other materials in cabinet being used:

a)  crayons

b)  paper - colored, plain, lined

c)  yarn

d)  pencils

VI.  Evaluation Procedures

1)  Students will be given a pen and pencil test with items taken from the knowledge objectives.

2)  Students will be evaluated through participation in group discussions.

3)  Students will be evaluated by their contributions in "Family Album."

4)  Students will be evaluated by writing a one-half page paper describing what their family means to them.

PART III: UNIT 3
EVALUATION OF SOCIAL STUDIES MATERIALS
Kenneth Craycraft

Upon entering the teaching field, many of you will be called upon to assist
in the evaluation of textbooks or other instructional materials.  While on the
surface this may seem like a rather easy task, it carries with it a great deal
of responsibility.  When it is considered that most materials are adopted for
periods of five to seven years, the integrity you exercise becomes even more
imperative.  Also, the interaction among and between the group selected is
critical.  A dominating individual can often sway a group to satisfy personal
bias.  To avoid such problems you whould have a guide to follow that allows for
individual as well as group involvement.

The following form allows for both subjective and objective evaluation of
social studies materials.  Your professor will provide copies from different
publishers of social studies materials and allow you time for examining and
rating each.

### SUGGESTIONS ON HOW TO USE THIS EVALUATION

The following evaluation instrument should be used as a guideline for
selecting social studies textbooks and materials.  The instrument will provide
a social studies staff with a common set of criteria.  In the past it was not
uncommon for each of the staff members to set up his/her own set of criteria
which, though allowing for individual differences in emphasis, did little to
promote the identification of common curriculum materials.  The instrument was
originally developed in the mid-1970's by elementary and secondary teachers, all
members of the Indiana Council for the Social Studies, with the intent of helping
all social studies teachers throughout the state use a common evaluation system.
The Council suggests that a local group may modify this evaluative criteria by
determining which items are crucial, establishing a weight system according to
the local objectives, or eliminating any items deemed inappropriate.

A Warning

The Council warns those using the instrument that final assessment according
to an average of items in a particular category or an average for all categories
may be misleading.  Probably the least effective use of this instrument would be
to examine all materials and compile an overall average for each set then rate
in a rank order, according to the averages.  A consistent rating of "1" on
particular items or categories might suggest certain in-service needs of a
staff rather than a weakness in the materials.

*QUESTIONS TO CONSIDER IN EVALUATING SOCIAL STUDIES MATERIALS

DIRECTIONS:    Circle the one number indicating the degree or extent of the question stated.  Add the total points circled in each category, and divide the total number by the number of items circled in each category.

KEY:    4 = Great Extent
    3 = Some Extent
    2 = No Extent
    1 = Unable to Judge

## DESCRIPTIVE CHARACTERISTICS

1. If you are a supporter of a multiple materials concept, to what extent do the materials being considered adequately meet this idea?    4  3  2  1

2. If there is a teacher's guide, to what extent do you believe it is generally useful?    4  3  2  1

3. A. If you believe an instructional strategy should be primarily inductive, to what extent are the materials appropriate?    4  3  2  1

   B. If you believe an instructional strategy should be primarily deductive, to what extent are the materials appropriate?    4  3  2  1

   C. If you believe both deduction and induction are essential to the instructional strategy, to what extent are the materials appropriate?    4  3  2  1

4. A. If you feel the recommended teacher behavior should be expository, to what extent are these materials applicable?    4  3  2  1

   B. If you feel the recommended teacher behavior should be a director of learning, to what extent are these materials applicable?    4  3  2  1

*Martha Lee, Robert Webb and Edward Poole.  "Suggested Evaluative Criteria for Social Studies Materials."  Published by the Indiana Council for the Social Studies.

DESCRIPTIVE CHARACTERISTICS   (continued)

C.  If you feel the recommended teacher behavior
to be something other than those mentioned
above, to what extent are these materials
applicable?                                          4    3    2    1

5.  If there are tests with the package, to what
extent are they applicable for general use in
your school?  (Be sure to consider instructional
techniques and approaches of your fellow faculty).   4    3    2    1

6.  To what extent are the author(s) and publisher
contributors to Social Studies education?            4    3    2    1

7.  To what extent have the materials been tested
by the author(s) prior to publication?               4    3    2    1

8.  To what extent do the field tests show favorable
results?                                             4    3    2    1

Total Points    _____

Descriptive Characteristics Average    _____

ANTECEDENT CONDITIONS

1.  To what extent would the program be successful
with each kind of pupil for whom the program is
considered?

    1)  Gifted                                       4    3    2    1

    2)  Average                                      4    3    2    1

    3)  Under Achievers                              4    3    2    1

    4)  Girls                                        4    3    2    1

    5)  Boys                                         4    3    2    1

    6)  Pupils who need highly structured
experiences                                  4    3    2    1

    7)  Pupils who can work without
supervision                                  4    3    2    1

2.  To what extent would each kind of pupil (for
whom this program is considered) be interested
in this program?

ANTECEDENT CONDITIONS  (continued)

| | | 4 | 3 | 2 | 1 |
|---|---|---|---|---|---|
| 8) | Gifted | 4 | 3 | 2 | 1 |
| 9) | Average | 4 | 3 | 2 | 1 |
| 10) | Under Achievers | 4 | 3 | 2 | 1 |
| 11) | Girls | 4 | 3 | 2 | 1 |
| 12) | Boys | 4 | 3 | 2 | 1 |
| 13) | Pupils who need highly structured experiences | 4 | 3 | 2 | 1 |
| 14) | Pupils who can work without supervision | 4 | 3 | 2 | 1 |

3. To what extent would the experiences and background of most teachers who will be using these materials in this school enable them to handle these materials effectively?　　　4　3　2　1

4. To what extent could in-service programs be used to remedy any teacher deficiencies in knowledge or skills?　　　4　3　2　1

5. To what extent will the community permit these types of materials to be used?　　　4　3　2　1

6. To what extent does your school have equipment that is essential to the use of the materials?

　　　(Consider such items as A.V. equipment, space available for large-small group instruction, adequate resource center, etc.)　　　4　3　2　1

Total Points　＿＿＿＿＿＿＿＿＿

Antecedent Conditions Average　＿＿＿＿＿＿＿＿＿

RATIONALE AND OBJECTIVES

1. To what extent does the program relate to the goals of your school system?　　　4　3　2　1

2. To what extent are the objectives stated in behavioral terms?　　　4　3　2　1

RATIONALE AND OBJECTIVES   (continued)

3.  To what extent does the program develop its
    stated objectives relative to:

|  |  |  |  |  |
|---|---|---|---|---|
| culture concepts | 4 | 3 | 2 | 1 |
| socialization | 4 | 3 | 2 | 1 |
| philosophical and religious | | | | |
| influences | 4 | 3 | 2 | 1 |
| ethnocentrism | 4 | 3 | 2 | 1 |
| geographic concepts | 4 | 3 | 2 | 1 |
| economic concepts | 4 | 3 | 2 | 1 |
| interdependence | 4 | 3 | 2 | 1 |
| political behavior concepts | 4 | 3 | 2 | 1 |
| change | 4 | 3 | 2 | 1 |

4.  To what extent does the program develop its
    stated objectives relative to:

|  |  |  |  |  |
|---|---|---|---|---|
| process of inquiry skills | 4 | 3 | 2 | 1 |
| psychomotor skills | 4 | 3 | 2 | 1 |
| developing attitudes and values | 4 | 3 | 2 | 1 |

Total Points   _____

Rationale and Objectives Average   _____

CONTENT

1.  To what extent is the subject matter rele-
    vant to the level of student for which the
    materials are being considered?                    4    3    2    1

2.  To what extent are the concepts developed
    (in those disciplines being considered)?

|  |  |  |  |  |
|---|---|---|---|---|
| anthropology | 4 | 3 | 2 | 1 |
| sociology | 4 | 3 | 2 | 1 |
| political science | 4 | 3 | 2 | 1 |
| economics | 4 | 3 | 2 | 1 |
| history | 4 | 3 | 2 | 1 |
| geography | 4 | 3 | 2 | 1 |
| social psychology | 4 | 3 | 2 | 1 |

CONTENT  (continued)

|  | philosophy | 4 | 3 | 2 | 1 |

3. To what extent does the program teach attitudes and values?  4  3  2  1

Total Points _____

Content Average _____

INSTRUCTIONAL THEORY AND TEACHING STRATEGIES

1. To what extent is the teaching strategy to be used explicitly stated?  4  3  2  1

2. To what extent does the program foster inquiry?  4  3  2  1

3. To what extent does the program design maintain proper teacher-pupil balance?  4  3  2  1

4. To what extent does the program develop concepts and generalizations?  4  3  2  1

5. To what extent does the program develop concepts and generalizations in a sequential and systematic way?  4  3  2  1

6. To what extent is there an acceptable variety and balance of teaching strategies?  4  3  2  1

7. To what extent does the program provide sufficient facts to support generalizations?  4  3  2  1

8. If the materials require one dominant teaching technique, to what extent is it desirable? (In terms of your staff, students, and acceptable techniques)?  4  3  2  1

Total Points _____

Instructional Theory and Teaching Strategies Average _____

MATERIALS

1. To what extent is each of the following
   available?  (Rate only those that are needed
   to fully implement these materials.)

| | |
|---|---|
| Background paper for the teachers | 4    3    2    1 |
| Supplemental materials for the pupil | 4    3    2    1 |
| Bibliography | 4    3    2    1 |
| Films | 4    3    2    1 |
| Filmstrips | 4    3    2    1 |
| Books | 4    3    2    1 |
| Slides | 4    3    2    1 |
| Magazine or Student Handouts | 4    3    2    1 |
| Transparencies | 4    3    2    1 |
| Realia or artifacts | 4    3    2    1 |
| Recordings | 4    3    2    1 |
| TV programs | 4    3    2    1 |
| Film loops | 4    3    2    1 |
| Other (list) | 4    3    2    1 |

Total Points _____

Materials Average _____

OVERALL JUDGMENTS

*1. To what extent do you believe these materials
    would be more effective than those you are
    currently using?                                   4    3    2    1

*2. To what extent would you rate these materials?

| | |
|---|---|
| effective | 4    3    2    1 |
| interesting | 4    3    2    1 |
| stimulating | 4    3    2    1 |
| meaningful | 4    3    2    1 |
| challenging | 4    3    2    1 |
| rewarding | 4    3    2    1 |

3. If these materials are being considered for
   general adoption, to what extent would you

<u>OVERALL JUDGMENTS</u>  (continued)

     recommend these materials for adoption for
general use in the department, i.e., by all
teachers?                                     4   3   2   1

4.  If the materials being examined are considered
for experimental use by a limited number of
teachers, to what extent would you recommend
these materials for adoption?                  4   3   2   1

5.  To what extent may these materials be used
without additional community involvement?      4   3   2   1

Total Points  _____

Overall Judgments Average  _____

*The opposites would show a low score.
That in itself should eliminate further consideration.

## CONCLUSION

Now that you have evaluated the material, do your results coincide with reviews that may have been published?  Check it out, and discuss the findings with the class.

Hopefully, this exercise has provided you with insight into some of the difficulties faced when evaluating textbook materials.  Remember, a textbook committee decision is important--especially since it involves both the teacher and the student for several years.  Finally, a textbook or textbook series represent only <u>one</u> source of information--do not forget this.

168

PART III: UNIT 4

"GIFTEDNESS IS A PROMISE, NOT A FACT"*

James L. Barth

As the title of this section suggests, "giftedness is a promise, not a fact." The children who are identified as gifted represent for the culture a promise of future superior performance. What schools have been asked to do is to intervene in what is conceived to be the normal process of education and identify those students who are gifted with special ability and to provide a special program.

Often giftedness is thought of as merely a demonstration of academic success. Students who score high on IQ, achievement and other kinds of standardized tests, as well as those who achieve in academic subject content, are thought to be "the gifted." However, that definition is much too narrow, for people are gifted with different kinds of special ability.

"Gifted and talented" may mean in school the exceptional athlete, the champion debater, the math whiz, the unusually mature student who organizes the fund raising for the junior class, and the student artist who designs the posters and prepares the backdrop for the school play. This group represents perhaps three percent, five percent, seven percent, of the student population. The percentage varies with the school system and with the desires of the school community. Normally gifted and talented represent a very small number of the students, from one to three percent. However, some communities in a desire to include a broader population have designated no less than one-quarter of their student body as gifted and talented. We do not want to argue here the merits ofsetting high or low identification percentages. It is perhaps enough to suggest that schools which are required to respond to local community pressures, may well find it convenient, if not desirable, to identify students in that community as fitting the criteria of gifted and talented who in a different school setting would not be so identified.

The gifted and talented program, as distrinct from other handicapped and equal opportunity programs, i.e., special education, compensatory disadvantaged programs, are seriously questioned by some teachers and parents. It is important to understand that many people in a community may resent and oppose the suggestion

_____

*This section on the gifted was originally published as part of a bulletin, Teaching Social Studies to the Gifted and Talented, Indiana Department of Public Instruction, by J. L. Barth and S. S. Shermis. It has been revised for purposes of this text.

that special programs should be provided for a very small, and from their point of view, elite group of students. It is, some maintain, undemocratic. It is alien to a system of equal opportunity. A system that identifies students who already have advantages over their peers is a system that is open to abuse. It takes no imagination to visualize the community's influential parents' wish that their children be identified as gifted and talented so that they might benefit from the special treatment. Also, it is true that school systems reward some kinds of giftedness but not others. The athletically-talented child is identified early and often given superior training, motivation and rewards. But other kinds of giftedness are not so esteemed. Within the last decade, it has become apparent to many that it is important--both to the society as a whole and to the development of the individual--that our society must be mobilized to identify, encourage and foster a much wider range of giftedness.

WHO ARE THE GIFTED AND TALENTED?

The definition of gifted and talented in use by the federal government and many state departments of public instruction is: The term "gifted and talented children" means children and, where applicable, youth, who are identified at the preschool, elementary or secondary level as possessing demonstrated or potential abilities that give evidence of high performance capability in areas such as intellectual, creative, specific academic, leadership, or in the performing and visual arts, and who, by reason thereof, require services or activities not ordinarily provided by the school.

The definition identifies five different categories of giftedness.

> The academically gifted frequently demonstrate specific academic aptitudes, i.e., they do very well in one or more areas such as science, mathematics, or literature.

> The intellectually gifted display a high level of generalized intellectual ability and frequently demonstrate outstanding performance in a diverse range of subject areas, i.e., they do very well in most areas of the school curriculum.

> The creatively gifted are capable of behavior and products which are unusual or original. Much of the time their products are divergent, that is, they depart from the usual or customary.

170

The <u>kinesthetically gifted</u> possess psychomotor talents or skills in visual or performing arts. That is, they do very well in painting, sculpture, dancing, the theatre arts, etc.

The <u>psycho-socially gifted</u> demonstrate clear evidence of leadership and qualitatively advanced ethical and moral development.

A word of caution: until now it has been difficult for even trained persons to identify the gifts of what is called mainstream children--white, middle class, already well motivated boys and girls. Identifying the talents of those who do not fit into this category is another story. For a variety of reasons, intellectually gifted Blacks, Mexican-Americans, Indians, economically disadvantaged and those with leadership and creative abilities have not proven to be quite as easy to identify. But again, the picture is changing. With better diagnostic tools, greater awareness of the diversity of giftedness and more understanding of the role played by culture in the development of the individual, it is increasingly easier to identify the gifted outside the mainstream of society.

CHARACTERISTICS OF THE FIVE CATEGORIES OF GIFTEDNESS

General Intellectual Ability

In general and with the usual precautions about exceptions, highly intelligent children possess a kind of generalized mental ability that manifests itself in an aptitude for problem-solving. Parents of gifted youngsters report that very early their gifted preschooler becomes absorbed in solving puzzles, riddles and mysteries. He/she begins reading--often before kindergarten--and persists in a book to the very end, because it is important to know how the story is resolved. With a rapidly growing supply of information and a consuming interest in all things, a gifted child is interested in solving problems at <u>different</u> <u>levels</u> of <u>abstraction</u>. That is, not only is a gifted child likely to converge on relatively simple questions such as: How do you spell "pithecanthropus"? What is the diet of dragonflies? And when did Charlemagne live? He/she usually begins to express interest in open-ended, often insolvable problems. Thus, long after the average child has put aside such questions as-- Where did the universe come from? Why is there so much injustice in the world-- gifted children continue to ask these questions.

## Specific Academic Aptitude

However, in some cases a particular intellectual gift may be limited and quite narrow. A child may be average or even well below average in most school subjects or skills but possess a talent of high order in, say, music, mathematics or technology. One author knows of an adolescent boy who was functionally illiterate but was nevertheless able to disassemble a modern automobile transmission, diagnose the problem and repair it. Another child, with a measured IQ of 70, was able to reproduce music with one hearing on the piano. These are extreme cases, however, and the generalization is that bright children are bright in most respects.

## Creative or Productive Thinking

Although the relationship between creativity and intellectual giftedness is by no means clear, perhaps because psychologists tend to use different measuring instruments, there does appear to be a relationship. Since 1950, when Guilford presented his now famous address before the American Psychological ASsociation, creativity and creative persons have been studied intensively. What exemplifies "creativity" or "creative behavior" is the production of truly novel, different, unique, and unexpected works. There is obviously a semantic problem here, for how "novel" or "different" must a work be before it is judged novel and different? And it is also often the case that enormously creative persons are not recognized until after their death. However, it is possible to identify language, poems, experiements, analyses, musical compositions, arguments and the like which are neither conventional nor customary. The very young child who spins a fully developed story out of his imagination, complete with exotic characters, strange locations and eccentric names is one case in point. So is the child who scorns blue skies, white clouds and green grass and prefers to paint multicolored skies and purple cows. Mendelssohn, although recognized as a musical prodigy, astounded everyone by writing a complete symphony at the age of seventeen. The poem "Thanatopsis," by William Cullen Bryant, which used to be in all American literature anthologies, is a haunting evocation of death and was also written by an adolescent of seventeen. An examination of novelists and poets will, in general, reveal a similar pattern: the young person preferred to read, write poetry or "play around" with words and ideas, often at a very early age. Needless to say, normal adults and children are often baffled by such strange doings, and sometimes the highly creative child finds his compansions' reactions strange or hostile.

## Leadership Ability

The older notion that a gifted child must necessarily be a homely, excentric loner should have evaporated when Lewis Terman began his pioneer work in the study of intelligence a half century ago. However, the stereotype persists despite the fact that research evidence shows just the opposite. Not only is it the case that highly intelligent young people tend to be slightly larger and better coordinated physically than the average, but there is also some evidence that they demonstrate leadership ability. The combination of superior physical endowment, imagination and persuasiveness somehow leads many able youngsters to become school officers, club presidents or the like. Such activities seem to provide an opportunity for talented young persons to learn leadership skills which serve as a means of influencing others. A study of the biographies of political, industrial and business leaders reveals with some consistency that such children become active leaders and that even preschoolers succeed in influencing those around them. Fortunately for society such children also tend to develop a higher degree of moral and ethical behavior when they could just as easily use their leadership skills for selfish or anti-social ends.

## The Kinesthetically Gifted

"Kinesthetics" is a term meaning "motion" or "movement." The "kinesthetically gifted" are, therefore, those who have a heightened ability in those activities which call for movement--the performing arts, the plastic arts, or athletics.

Those with ability in the visual or performing arts tend to provide early evidence of aptitude for rhythm, dancing or other coordinated movements. They are typified by those who start in gymnastics as a five-or-six-year-old, and eventually are selected for an Olympics gymnastics team.

The same generalizations are appropriate for the musically or artistically gifted. Those with musical or artistic gifts usually signal their talents early by being able to clap in rhythm, reproduce tune by voice, teach themselves to play instruments or--as in the case of Mozart and a few others--teach themselves musical notation and begin to compose. Those with artistic talent often naturally gravitate toward crayons, pastel chalks, paints, and the like and soon begin to experiment and invent. Their early productions are often noteworthy for dramatic uses of color or other signs of striking individuality. Often the artistically gifted provide other evidence of their talents by collecting works of art, reproductions, records, and books, and by nagging their parents for visits to art museums.

Teachers often report that even first and second grade children who are kinesthetically gifted move with more grace than normal children. They soon move out of the awkward and jerky stage and begin to make movements that are precise and poised. One author knows of a child who began the study of karate at the age of eleven. Although only about half the size of the other students, he soon mastered the complex and difficult movements and began to pass the test. Within two months he had made it to "yellow," a notch above beginner's grade. One can say much the same about those who become competitive or professional athletes. They provide early indications of kinesthetic talent by excelling in school football, baseball or basketball teams. They are also the ones who are able to learn athletic skills rapidly--often with incredible rapidity. Babe Didrikson Zaharias was able to break par within a few days of picking up her first golf club.

Although there are exceptions to every generalization about the gifted, creative and talented there are, nevertheless, certain statements which most researchers agree are generally true. For instance, gifted children seem to possess a generalized intellectual ability, although many are rather specifically endowed, that is, have talents in only one or two areas. Often their language, ideas or tangible productions are characterized by being creative, different, unique, or unusual. They often demonstrate leadership ability and, despite the ancient stereotype, are often larger and better physically endowed than the average. Those who are kinesthetically gifted can perform psychomotor activities with grace and fluidity and are likely to do well in the performing arts and athletics.

This section on characteristics of the gifted is concluded by briefly enumerating some behaviors which, while not inevitable, usually signal the presence of giftedness or considerable talent.

## POSSIBLE GIFTED BEHAVIORS

### Complexity

Intellectually gifted children are attracted to complex problems. They are able to conceptualize a complicated situation, see the distinction between two nearly identical things, suggest a wide range of hypotheses, and explain logical processes. The musically gifted child, for example, soon tires of nursery rhymes and become interested in the more complex musical compositions.

## Wide-ranging Interests

One of the most dependable signs of giftedness is the child's early and insatiable curiosity about everything. Parents of gifted children frequently have their patience taxed for they tire of answering one question after another, literally hour after hour. The gifted child's alertness and curiosity are often manifested at the toddler stage. These are likely to develop into reading, collecting, watching, and seeking behaviors.

## Fund of Information

Because of the gifted child's alertness and continuing curiosity, such children soon develop an extraordinarily large fund of information--the result of constant observing, reading, talking, and analyzing. This is why the daily conversations of very gifted children have an almost unearthly quality about them; while their information and understanding are likely to be skewed and distorted, the very fact that an eight-year-old knows anything at all about animals of the Mesozoic period or the characteristics of a Da Vinci portrait is likely to unsettle adults.

## Risk-taking

Many gifted children manifest an urge to take risks. To them, the conventional, ordinary or customary approach is dull. Risk-taking can be seen in the unexpected question, "How come, if Columbus found Indians in the New World, we don't say that the Indians discovered America?" It is evident in their willingness to learn a new skill, play a new game, see a different part of the world, read a book that is judged "too difficult." The courage to try something new, therefore, is linked with the already discussed creativity and seems often to be an important part of the gifted child's repertoire of behavior.

## Conclusion

Whether a particular gifted child will eventually develop one or all of his/her talents is the question. As Avner Ziv, Israeli educational psychologist, asserts through his work, giftedness is a promise, not a fact (Counseling the Intellectually Gifted Child. New York: Columbia Teachers College, 1977). A gifted child poses a promise of things to come. Initially, a gifted child is not a fully functioning, fulfilled and developed person. Under the best of circumstances, a gifted child's potentialities and promises will reach fruition. But the best of circumstances does not always happen. Of course, when children fail to reach potentional, there are likely to be social factors other than the school involved. Sometimes the peer group deliberately represses signs of intellectual giftedness; sometimes parents fail to recognize abilities; sometimes the gifted child simply does not want to expend the effort. Poverty and the struggle for existence leave children too tired and depleted to care. In some cases a succession of emotional conflicts erodes talent. However, teachers armed with the ability to identify both the different categories of giftedness and the characteristics of the gifted, with appropriate techniques and materials, can broaden the intellectual range of their classrooms and can vitalize their classrooms to be places of joy and growth for gifted and talented children.

PART III:  UNIT 5

Mainstreaming in the Social Studies Classroom:  A Renewed Challenge*

Larry Dean Wills

As a result of Public Law 94-142, a new term has emerged, and that is "Mainstreaming."  Prior to this law, students who had some form of learning handicap were generally placed with special education teachers and separated from the regular classroom teacher and students.  Now that the regular classroom teacher may have students who have some form of learning difficulty, it becomes necessary for the teacher to be aware of accommodating strategies which may be appropriate for the handicapped learner.  The purpose of this section is to acquaint you with some techniques which might help you when working with the mainstreamed student.

Regular classroom teachers often fear mainstreaming because they do not understand "jargon" being used by special education teachers, and they conclude that special educators know much about teaching they do not.  Once one has become conversant with the language, the problem takes on a different dimension.   J. Herlihy and M.Herlihy have noted, "Mainstreaming is a difficult concept to reduce to a definition.  It is more an attitude or value-oriented position that allows the teacher to examine each child and provide an appropriate way to develop, expand, and refine the student's intellectual, social, and emotional skills."[1]

The regular classroom teacher is not alone in implementing mainstreaming. The intent of P.L. 94-142 is that "...educators should have the knowledge and skills necessary to enable them to respond to the individual differences of learners."[2]  General and special educators must work as a team to ensure all handicapped students are placed with non-handicapped students as much as possible. Testing and evaluation should be non-discriminatory, and individualized plans should be developed for each handicapped student.

---

*This section was originally published in American Secondary Education, "Mainstreaming in Secondary Schools," Special Issue, Vol. 12, 1982.  It has been revised for purposes of this text.

Since this is a team effort, the knowledge and skills of the special educator will relieve the regular teacher of many tasks required by the mainstreaming legislation. For example, the due process safeguards, non-discriminatory testing and evaluation, and basic construction of the I.E.P.'s will remain largely in the domain of the special educator and support personnel. The regular education teacher should have a voice in the construction of the I.E.P.; however, the major task of the classroom teacher is to work with the handicapped student in the regular classroom.

Throughout your social studies methods course, you have been exposed to a number of techniques which can be used with the mainstreamed student. You are, therefore, well on your way to working with your special students. We should, however, highlight some of the techniques with which you are familiar when working with the mainstreamed student. Kenworthy offers the following suggestions:[3]

1) Have a variety of textbooks, and help pupils find ones they can read and understand the best;

2) Arrange for a variety of activities, not all of them reading, so that the slower students will not always be handicapped by their reading difficulties;

3) Include as many visual aids as possible;

4) Ask the slower pupils the least difficult questions, and save the more searching questions for the bright students;

5) Try to arrange for varied homework, some reading and some non-reading activities;

6) Encourage pupils and praise them when they do something well;

7) Conduct supervised study, and spend most of your time with the slower students;

8) Work in pairs so faster students can help slower ones;

9) Encourage role-playing and dramatics, in which slower students can often excel.

Another teaching strategy with which you may be familiar is content selection. To assist in this process, the regular classroom teacher can employ what is termed "content analysis." Here the teacher decides which

material from a particular text is most important for the students. With
content analysis, the course material is divided into three major headings:
facts, concepts, and generalizations. When a teacher can recognize the
major generalizations and concepts in a text, selecting content becomes simplified.
The educator does not simply go from page to page or chapter to chapter. Instead, the major generalizations are identified, concepts which support the
generalizations are taught, and only those facts which are needed to form
the concepts are emphasized.

Once the text has been analyzed, the teacher underlines these major
generalizations, concepts, and facts inthe text for the student who has reading
difficulties. Students then read those selections of the text which relate
directly to the major objectives of the unit. Irrelevant information is therefore eliminated, and the student concentrates reading time on the major parts
of the chapter. Content analysis thus enables the teacher to emphasize the most
important parts of the text and eliminate the embellishments which may distract
the less able reader.

Also emphasized in regular methods courses is expository teaching. McKenzie
outlines four general principles to be followed in the expository approach.[4]
Briefly, the strategy is as follows:

1) Work with students to achieve a certain goal. As an introductory
   activity for a lesson, the teacher informs the students what
   they are to learn to do. When students are aware of what is
   expected, they become less confused and frustrated; failure is
   reduced.

2) Eliminate or reduce irrelevant stimuli. McKenzie suggests
   keeping lectures brief and to the point, telling students
   what paragraphs relate directly to the topic being discussed,
   and having them skip irrelevant readings.

3) Organize information with cues. Once again, content analysis is
   a prerequisite to this task. First, highlight the important
   information. For example, McKenzie recommends the teacher set
   off key ideas in special print. During a lecture, name the
   principles or main ideas and write them on the chalkboard.

Second, subordinate ideas to each other to show relationships. On a bulletin board or chalkboard, the teacher may place the generalization on top with connecting lines to show which are to be discussed and learned. In this way, the students can see where the discussion is going and how what has been covered relates to what is being currently discussed. In essence, this is a structured overview of the day's lesson, and can also be constructed for an entire unit.

4) Elicit frequent responses from all individuals. When constructing a lesson plan, the teacher identifies key points in the lesson. Then, the teacher plans a question that requires students to recall or apply each key idea. According to McKenzie, the teacher then plans a means by which every pupil can indicate an answer or show a response by a simple nonverbal gesture the teacher can interpret as right or wrong. This way, the student is not singled out for a wrong answer.[4]

The techniques and strategies listed above are not really new, and you should be able to employ them with students who have been mainstreamed in your class. Perhaps mainstreaming will enable us to remember that all students are different and their learning styles are different. Whether we are working with a regular or special student, we sould recognize that each deserves special consideration.

---

1.  J. Herlihy, and M. Herlihy, eds. Mainstreaming in the Social Studies, (National Council for Social Studies: Bulletin 62, 1980).

2.  National Council for Accreditation of Teacher Education, (Washington, D. C., 1980).

3.  Kenworthy, L. Guide to Social Studies Teaching, (Wadsworth, 1973), 124-127.

4.  G. McKenzie. "How to Increase the Odds that Pupils Will Learn What You Mean to Teach," The Social Studies, 1980, 270-273.

PART III:  UNIT 6

Multicultural and Global Education in the Social Studies Classroom

Perry Marker

July 20, 1969.  From a global perspective, it was a date that forever changed how we look at ourselves.  It was the capstone of an extraordinary effort of technology and ingenuity that spanned a decade.  When Commander Neil A. Armstrong took "one small step" on the lunar surface we gained a whole new perspective of ourselves.  The photographs of our tiny planet, floating in the blackness of space, that astronauts beamed back from over a quarter million miles away graphically illustrated the true global nature of this place we call Earth.

Today, the global issues and problems we face are diverse:  hunger, poverty, the struggle for world peace, conservation of our natural resources and pollution of our environment are but a few of the concerns that effect everyone on our planet.  With these highly complex problems come concerns about how we live that will shape our lives for generations.  It would indeed be unfortunate if we, as social studies teachers, fail to help our students face these problems in this increasingly complex and interdependent world.

Ours is a highly interdependent world composed of many different cultures and ethnic groups.  Television, jet travel and satellite communication have brought all of us closer together and has increased our awareness that we all share common interests but also have distinctively different customs, traditions and lifestyles.

## CHANGING CONCEPTIONS OF OUR CULTURE

For many years, it was popular to speak of America as "the great melting pot."  Immigrants from other countries were expected to acquire the language and customs of the "American" culture and reject their own traditions, language and culture.  Often people were ridiculed if they did not make the transition to the "American" way of life.  Many believed that this blending of cultures into one distinctively "American" culture increased our sense of national unity and nationalistic spirit.

Today, our society is composed of many different groups. Blacks, Hispanics, Poles, Italians, Germans, Japanese and Chinese all make up our culture. The cultural traditions and customs of these groups add to our society, making it unique. Evidence of these groups can be found all over our country; urban and rural areas alike reflect this diversity. In many communities evidence of cultural diversity can be found in architecture, restaurants, and many other businesses. The presence of this cultural diversity is recognized as a strength. Rather than a melting pot, America can be seen as a "tossed salad." Just as a salad is composed of many different ingredients adding their own special flavor to the whole salad, such is the nature of our society with each of the various ethic groups contributing to a national culture while maintaining their own distinct identity.

In your own community, what evidence of other cultures can you find? What is the origin of this influence? How does it contribute to your community?

## WHAT IS MULTICULTURAL/GLOBAL EDUCATION?

Multicultural/global education has been widely discussed in the educational literature. Unfortunately, there is little agreement as to a precise definition of these concepts. Both are distinct, yet related. For our discussion, multicultural and global education will be discussed in terms of their major goals and purposes and how they are related.

The primary purpose of multicultural education is to promote a respect for a wide range of cultrual groups within our society. Within the context of multicultural education, all cultural groups can experience equal social, economic and educational opportunities. Multicultural education affirms that cultural diversity is a valuable resource that should be preserved, experienced and extended. Multicultural education is concerned with teaching about cultural diversity that exists in our society.

Global education views the many cultures of our planet as interacting and interdependent. Global education goes beyond our society and recognizes that nations and peoples of the world are closely linked through ethnic heritage, religion, communications, trade, monetary systems, science and many other sources. Global education is concerned with developing global identifications and the knowledge, skills and attitudes needed for students to become effective world citizens. Global education assumes that there are many different points of view or perspectives among the world's cultures and that living in today's world is a matter of living in a global community.

Given these differences, multicultural and global education share some common concerns. These common purposes can help to shape a social studies curriculum that emphasizes multicultural/global education. (1) Both seek to:

- improve interpersonal and intergroup relations;

- increase the awareness of the impact of global and national trends, institutions on different ethnic groupings of people;

- reduce stereotyping and increase intergroup understanding;

- help students comprehend the significance of human diversity;

- improve intercultural understanding.

Multicultural education focuses on cultural diversity in our society. Global education is concerned with interdependence and intercultural communication between and among world cultures. Multicultural and global education have common goals. These shared goals are central to developing a multicultural/ global education curriculum in the social studies classroom.

HOW DOES MULTICULTURAL/GLOBAL EDUCATION FIT IN THE SOCIAL STUDIES CLASSROOM?

Today, more than any other time in history, citizenship requires consideration of global, national, state and local conditions and relationships. Social studies educators who incorporate multicultural and global concepts in the classroom must seek to develop the knowledge, skills and values necessary for effective interpersonal communication, decision making and participation. In a classroom that emphasizes the importance of multicultural/global education, students learn how the world, its cultures, ethnic groups and various institutions function. Students develop critical thinking skills that can be used to understand and relate to their complex world.

How people in our country and around the world live affects us. We constantly come into contact with the world on a daily basis. Whether at your local grocer or favorite stereo dealer, products from other countries and cultures are commonplace. Stop and look at items you have in your possession. How many are made domestically? What items are imported? From what different countries are these from?